JAPANESE FAIRY TALES

JAPANESE FAIRY TALES

J. ROBERT MAGEE

YOHAN PUBLICATIONS, INC.

JAPANESE FAIRY TALES

First printing April 1995

Copyright © 1995 by J. Robert Magee

Illustrated by
KAZUMASA MIYAMOTO
HIROKO KANZAKI

YOHAN PUBLICATIONS, INC.
14-9, Okubo 3-chome, Shinjuku-ku, Tokyo, Japan.

Printed in Japan

Contents

Kitsune Nyōbō—The Fox Wife　1

Dancing For Demons—Kobutori Jiisan　13

The Man Who Brought the Dead Back
to Life　24

Kasa Jizō, or Kindness Repaid　39

Momotarō, the Peach Boy　48

Kintarō, the Young Atlas　71

Sannen Netarō—Japan's Rip Van Winkle　87

Urashima Tarō and the World Below　100

Hanasaka Jiisan　123

Kaguyahime—Moon Princess Born from
Bamboo　141

Japanese Terms and Expressions　161

Note: Japanese folk tales are full of stories where animal transform themselves into human form. Sometimes these are evil animals changing shape to hurt humans, and sometimes these are good animals with more noble intentions.

Kitsune Nyōbō —The Fox Wife

LONG ago there was a small, lonely house deep in the mountains of Northern Japan. The house was home to a hunter, who kept himself fed with rabbits, birds and other game he took from the mountains and forests around him.

As you might expect from a man living all alone deep in the mountains in what was already one of the more sparsely populated parts of Japan, the hunter's life was hand-to-mouth; if he could not find and kill a nice bird, a juicy rabbit, or some other beast, he would have nothing to eat save some of the meager vegetables from his garden.

One late autumn day, much like any other, the man was hunting in the woods for his supper. He alternated his hunting grounds regularly, and on this particular day he was hunting on a mountain called Shinoda-ga-mori.

The hunter could sense something was not right with the world. For weeks now he had noticed there were fewer animals in the woods than usual. Flocks of geese, ducks and other birds still flew by, but these were fewer, and there were fewer birds in the flocks than before. Fewer rabbits stumbled into the hunter's snares, and he hadn't come across a wild boar in longer than he could remember. "Where have all the animals gone?" he wondered to himself.

1

As the man climbed the mountain, watching the trails for signs of a fresh trail, he came to a mountain stream. On the far bank of the stream, the hunter saw a fox.

Foxes don't make for good eating. There's not a lot of meat, and if a hunter has his choice, he'll take a rabbit or a bird any day. But these were not normal times. Our hunter had not eaten in several days and was starting to wonder when he would find his next meal. "A fox isn't a lot of meat, but it's better than no meat at all," he thought. "And the fur will be good with winter coming on. It'll do."

Like the hunter, the fox was looking a bit hungry and thin. Still, it was a magnificent fox. Its coat was thick and the tail was a deep red, proof it had seen many winters on this mountain. Slowly, quietly, he raised his matchlock.

The fox was drinking water from the stream, and hadn't sensed the danger awaiting it. It kept lapping at the stream as the hunter brought his weapon to bear. But just before the man pulled the trigger, the fox looked up at him. The hunter hesitated, and the fox slowly sat back on its haunches. As it did this, it looked straight at the hunter and brought both forepaws together as if it were praying, begging the hunter to spare it.

The man was an experienced hunter, well versed in the ways of animals and things wild. But he had never met an animal that begged for its life. The hunter knew all he had to do was pull the trigger and supper was his, plus a warm fur for the cold months ahead. But the fox seemed to know this too, and that somehow moved the hunter's spirit just enough to cause him to lower his sights and wave the fox away.

The fox made a quick bow, then disappeared into the brush. The hunter thought of the old fox and his red tail, and wondered what he had just done. Then his stomach grumbled at him, and he remembered what he had to do.

Darkness began to fall shortly after the hunter left the stream. He went home empty handed, and sat before his fire drinking *sake* and eating the last of his vegetables.

Just as the sun dropped behind the mountains there was a knock at the door. This startled the man, for he was alone in his part of the mountains. An occasional wood-cutter would pass through, or a fugitive from the law, but most of these were solitary types. He had few visitors.

He opened the door and found there, much to his surprise, a woman. A very attractive woman, alone and carrying only a single cloth knapsack.

"*Konban wa*," she said. "Good evening."

"Good evening," the hunter replied cautiously.

"I seem to have lost my way," she said. "I couldn't find the right trail, then it got too dark to find my way at all."

The man said nothing.

"Do you think I could stay here?"

The man was lonely. He himself had chosen this life of solitude deep in the mountains, but he was human and at times he longed for someone to talk with. Here, on a cold night in the mountains, he had company. And a lady at that.

The man hesitated. "I have no food to offer her," he thought. "How can I have guests if I can't treat them properly. How do I treat them? I haven't had a proper guest in, ah, oh, a long time. But it's been so long since I've had someone to talk to."

"It's cold out. Please, come in," he said.

She was on her way to visit relatives in the town on the far side of the mountains. There was a path connecting the woman's town and the other town, but it went around the mountains and took several days. She had hoped to cut through the mountains and make it to the town in just a day or two, but the mountains proved much more rugged than she had expected.

"I'm afraid I have nothing to offer you but a few vegetables and some *sake*," the man said apologetically.

"I have food here," she pointed to her knapsack. "We can eat this. It was for my relatives, but I didn't expect to be caught here like this. Please, have some."

And almost instantly, she had prepared a plate full of food for the hunter. Wonderful food: rabbit, fowl, even some sweet potatoes for a dessert. The man ate very little at first, but as he ate, the woman refilled his plate so that no matter how much he ate there was always more!

The two talked as they ate, and the man remembered how nice it was to have company.

They talked late into the night. On rising, the woman looked around the hunter's tiny mountain home. She looked out the window at the mountains surrounding them, and at the forest, and at the stream.

"This is a nice place," she told him. "It's so peaceful. Would you mind if I stayed a little longer?"

Of course he didn't mind.

A little while became a little while longer, and the two grew closer. Days became months, and months slipped into years. The two lived happily. Eventually, the woman found she was with child. Soon she gave birth to the hunter's son.

Early one hot summer day, the hunter found his prey and started back for his tiny home. Things were better now, he thought. The animals were back in his traps and on the trails. He and the woman and baby Dojimaru had plenty of meat. With the woman's help, the man's meager garden had grown to include more and different kinds of plants.

As the man rounded a bend on the mountain path, he came to a point where the trail overlooked his tiny home. He looked down at his home and saw the woman on the porch, nursing their son. But what he also saw was a tail! The woman had a tail like a fox-tail, and she was thump-thump-thumping it on the floor of the porch to cool herself in the summer heat!

Seeing this all from far up the mountain, the man looked again. And there again was the red tail thumpitty-thumping on the porch.

His mind reeled. "It's that fox! The one I saved," he thought. "It changed into a woman. It must take me for a fool because I saved its life. And after all this time..."

The man stormed down the path and roared up to the porch. "Take a bath!" he yelled.

"But, the child—"

"I'll take care of the child," he said, taking the child from her arms. "You take a bath. Now!"

Foxes don't enjoy baths very much, and the hunter wanted to see if the woman would really enter the bath. Her refusal would prove, in his mind, that she was the fox transformed into a woman.

But she did not refuse. Not suspecting that he had discovered her secret from upon the mountain, she obeyed him and went to the bath.

Before long the man heard the splish-splash-splursh of water from the bath. He set down the child and walked around the house to the bath. He looked closely at the walls, trying to find a crack or knothole large enough to see through. He was not a dirty old man—he had built the house when he was living alone—but he knew his carpentry was not perfect. Eventually he found what he was looking for—a small gap between the planks. He looked through and saw that the splish-splash of water in the bath was only the woman slapping her tail on the surface of the tub. She was using her tail to make it sound as if she were taking a bath herself, but she hadn't even removed her clothes.

She *was* a fox, he decided. She had transformed herself into human form. She had deceived him every day and every night for the past year, no, two, no, how—many years?

On seeing the woman's tail with his own eyes, the man became very angry. But he had loved her. And even though he was irate with her for deceiving him, he couldn't hate her for it. He still loved her.

It was the thought of the child that brought out his deepest rage. "How could she do this to a child?" he wondered when he thought of the child's future. The child was normal, human in all aspects. But the man knew that if anyone ever discovered his mother's secret, the child was doomed to a life of mistrust, whispers and cruel animal jokes behind his back.

He played out scenes in his mind:

"There goes the wolf-boy."

"Hey, fox-child. Was that you in our chicken pen last night?"

"Want some raw meat for lunch, foxy?"

The man's eyes pressed into the back of his head with anger.

He started giving the child pointers to make sure his lineage would not be discovered. He taught the child, but, realizing the boy was much too young to understand some things, he wrote his lessons out in a notebook.

I.   Never step on the railing that divides *tatami* mats in door and the entranceway to the outside. People are superstitious about this. Also, be careful about stepping on the edge of *tatami* mats.

II. Do not chase butterflies, dragon flies or other insects. Foxes and other animals may do this, but people do not.

III. Never gulp your food. Some people do this, but it is a sign of bad manners.

IV. ....

When he had written all the lessons he could think of, he turned to the fox. She was completely in human form.

"I am The Fox of Shinoda-ga-mori," she said.

"This is repayment for the time I saved your life?"

"No. I repaid you, but that was long ago. I gave you food to eat in place of my own flesh. I stayed with you because you were so lonely, living all here by yourself. Not even you realized how lonely you were." Tears welled up in her eyes.

"I have given you a child," she said, maintaining her composure. "Please take care of him. I will return to Shinoda-ga-mori."

And the next day, when the man was out hunting the day's meal, the fox returned to the woods. She left the child and a note written on the wall.

> *If the child cries and cries and won't stop,*
> *bring him to Shinoda-ga-mori.*
> *If you have troubles with the child,*
> *bring him to Shinoda-ga-mori.*
> *Please take care of him.*

Nothing more.

Before too long, the baby sensed his mother was gone. He began to cry, *"Kaa-chan* (Mommy)! *Kaa-chan!"* He wailed for hours without end. He cried all day and all night, and on the second day of crying the father decided it would be better to visit Shinoda-ga-mori.

The man carried Dojimaru to the mountain, with the child blubbering all the way. *"Kaa-chan! Kaa-chan!"*

As they reached the edge of the mountain they heard the swish-a-swish of something coming through the grasses. Soon the swishing grew louder, and a fox poked its head from a crook between two trees.

Dojimaru saw his mother in her true form, but he had never seen a fox before. He was frightened! He stopped crying and jumped behind his father. *"Too-chan* (Daddy)*! Save me!"* he yelled.

The hunter understood this was part of the fox's plan to stop the child from searching for his mother. He also understood her pain as she watched her child hide from her in fear.

Dojimaru never asked for his mother again.

The father and son returned to their home in the mountains. The boy had a normal childhood, but when the hunter began to teach him to read and write, he discovered the boy learned with amazing speed. Where normal children

his age could learn only a few Chinese characters a month, Dojimaru could learn dozens. Where normal boys had trouble with basic addition and subtraction, Dojimaru soon grew bored with multiplication and division. Clearly, he had inherited his mother's foxy quick-wittedness.

It soon became clear that Dojimaru had also inherited beauty and grace far superior to normal humans. These attributes made his climb to success quick. Before long Dojimaru was able to provide for his father so well that the man could live an easy life in the mountains. The man lived his days in the shadow of Shinoda-ga-mori, hunting only when he wanted, and then only for sport, not necessity.

Kitsune is Japanese for "fox". *Nyōbō* means "wife".

Dancing For Demons—
Kobutori Jiisan

T HERE once was a man with a lump on his face.
Of course, there are many men and women with
lumps on their faces, but this man's lump was
much larger than you might expect.

The lump first made itself known when the
man was ten years old. When it started, it was
about the size of a golf ball, but it grew and grew
over the years until it became the size of a
mikan, or a small orange.

His parents didn't think much of it at first,
but they came to realize it might cause their son
some problems when the time came for him to
find a bride. They talked with the local wise
men, traveled to the city to consult with doctors,
bought snake-oil remedies and magic charms
from traveling salesmen, but nothing they did
had any effect on the *mikan*-sized lump.

The man lived a good life, and eventually
found a wonderful wife who loved him despite
the lump on his face. The man did many good
deeds for the people in his little village. But the
lump on his face made him different from the
rest of the villagers, and it seems people are always suspicious of those who stand out from the
crowd. No matter how generous he was, the villagers would always gossip about him when his
back was turned.

Their speculation knew no bounds. "It's a second head, you know. Yes. His mother thought she was going to have twins. When she gave birth, one of the babies was born without a head, and the other one had *two* heads!"

"He must have done something terrible in a former life," said others. "The lump must be his punishment."

One day the man was out cutting firewood in the hills around the village. He had just finished cutting the wood and bundling it to carry back when it started to rain.

He looked around for a place to keep out of the rain, but the only thing he found was an old, hollowed out tree trunk. He crawled into the trunk and waited for the shower to pass.

But the shower did not pass. It grew stronger and more violent with each passing moment until it because a full-fledged thunderstorm. Lightning flashed across the sky as the rain pounded on the man's shelter. "This could go on all night," the man worried.

But the storm ended shortly before sunset. The old man crept from his shelter and looked around the hills. He could probably gather his wood and make it home just as it got dark.

He grumbled to himself as he gathered the wood. "Wet wood. Can't make a fire with this till it dries. How will I heat the house tonight?"

Before long, he heard voices off in the distance. He went to the edge of the hill and looked down the path to see who could be coming. It was a band of demons—hundreds of them!

He saw ogres, monsters, demons and devils of all sorts coming down the path—right toward him! He jumped up and ran back to his hollow. He grabbed some of the wood he had gathered and climbed into the trunk, pulling the wood over opening in the trunk to hide himself.

He heard the monsters singing as they came closer to his tree. But the singing didn't fade away as the demons passed by the man's tree. The demons did not pass by his tree. When the man peeked through a crack in the wood, he saw that the demons had stopped on his hillside. They were having a feast!

Some monsters were building a spit for

roasting meat ("What kind of meat?" wondered the man.), others were passing around huge flagons of mead and ale, and some others were playing some gambling game with dice.

A few demons began to dance to what to the man sounded like the most horrible music ever heard. The devils in the orchestra were playing instruments that looked normal, but the sounds they produced were the worst tortures imaginable: grating, piercing noises like fingernails on chalkboards and cats wailing on hot summer nights.

The merriment continued until the man, forgetting himself in the excitement and merriment around him, stepped out from his hiding place. In the midst of the celebration, with dancing, singing, gambling and so on all around him, the man was able to wander around the festival unmolested, if not unnoticed.

Just outside his tree, the man saw a raised platform. On the platform was a demon larger than most of the others. His clothes look particularly fine, and the man assumed this was the throne of the chief of the demons. But the man was puzzled to see that the demon chief looked patently bored, even depressed with the celebration around him.

"Your dance is most boring," the chief said to a group of monsters before him. "Is there no one here who can entertain me?"

The chief of the demons then looked around at

his celebration. When he came to the man with the lump on his face, the demon king smiled.

"And who are you?" he asked. "You are not one of us. Will you provide us with a little entertainment?" A wry smile crossed his devilish lips. "Or will you provide us with our dinner?"

The man gulped. But instead of running, or begging for his life, the man gathered up his courage and said, "I shall dance."

Aside from the lump on his face and his various acts of kindness, the man was also well known in his village as an accomplished dancer. He was untrained, and followed none of the accepted styles of the day, but his grace and emotion were exceptional.

The man was confident in his abilities. But he was also a bit nervous, for he knew he was

gambling with his life. If his dancing displeased the demon chief, there would be hell to pay.

The rest of the merry-makers grew quiet and all eyes turned to the man. At the chief's signal, the demon orchestra struck up a tune and the man began to dance.

At first, his fear made his movements were awkward. But he soon found his confidence and danced as never before.

When the dance was over, the chief of the demons stood and saluted him. "Most entertaining, good sir. Most entertaining," he said. "Come and join me in a cup of mead."

Breathless, the man took a seat on the chief's raised platform. The demon passed him a cup. "You are a most exceptional dancer," he praised the man. "I can't recall the last time I was this entertained by a dancer, demon or human. Most captivating. Please, help yourself to something to eat."

Soon, the party drew to a close. The demon asked his dancer, "You must come and perform for us again."

"How could I refuse any invitation from you?"

"How, indeed. But you must leave us with more than your word. We must have something you value."

Cleverly, the man put his hand to his face as if to cover the lump there. "But I have nothing of value."

A demon aide leaned over and whispered to his chief. "Look! See how he tries to hide the lump on his face! He must prize that highly."

The chief whispered a reply, then turned again to the man. "You give yourself away, sir. We want the lump on your face. Leave it with us as a gesture that you will return tomorrow and perform for us again."

Before the man could reply, the demon chief had plucked the lump from his face as if it had never been there at all. He tossed it in the air like a ball and said, "We will return it when we see you tomorrow night."

The man touched his cheek as he walked home down the hilly path. His right cheek, where the lump had been, was as smooth as his left. Indeed, it was as if he had never had such a lump at all!

He hurried home and told his family his amazing story. No one could doubt him, for his lump truly was gone and there could be no other explanation.

After the man had told his story, one of his servants was talking with a cook from the house next door. The neighbor was a very cranky old man who also had a lump on his face. Unlike his now lumpless neighbor, the cranky old man had let the lump on his face cloud his personality. The blemish angered him, and he hated everyone around him for his own imperfection.

The servant told the cook how his master

had lost his lump. "Maybe your master could do the same, the old sourpuss. Ha, ha," the servant joked.

"If only he could dance," laughed the cook.

The cook went and told his master of his neighbor's good fortune. The cranky old man was very happy to hear the story. Of course, he was not happy for his neighbor's good fortune; he was happy because he saw a chance to get rid of his own lump.

The cranky neighbor dressed quickly and paid a call on his neighbor. He listened with glee as his neighbor recounted his tale. When the story was done, he asked, "Of course, you will not return there tomorrow night?"

"I don't want my lump back, and I would rather not entertain demons any more."

"Perhaps I could go in your place?" suggested the cranky neighbor. "Dancing for demons seems a small price to pay to get rid of this lump."

The good neighbor agreed and explained how to find the picnic site and what time to go, what to expect and so on. The cranky neighbor listened intently, and when he had learned all he needed to know he returned to his home.

The next afternoon, the cranky old man went out to the hills in search of the hollow and the clearing. When he found the right tree, he climbed in and waited for the demons to return.

The demons came at the agreed-upon time

and began their merriment as before. The man watched from the tree as the celebration grew, and more and more demons joined the festivities.

Finally, he summoned up his courage and stepped from his hiding place.

"There you are," said the chief demon. "We've been waiting for you. Come, dance for us."

The man stood before the demon chief and smiled weakly. By nature a cranky old man, he had devoted little time to enjoying himself. Entertainments such as dancing or singing were completely alien to him, and now he was asked to perform for others? To give pleasure to others?

The hellish chorus began their song again and the man began to writhe. He wiggled this way and that as he imitated what he thought of as dancing, but his attempts pleased no one.

The demon chief was most disappointed, and did not invite the man to join the feast.

"Your dancing yesterday was most entertaining, but today something seems lacking. We are most disappointed."

The man shook with fear at the thought of becoming a new entertainment for the demons.

The demon chief was unhappy, but he remembered his delight with the previous day's performance.

"We will not kill you," he said as he reached into the folds of his robe. "However, we no longer require this."

Before the failed dancer could move, the demon had pulled out the kind old man's lump and attached it to the left side of the old man's face. "Leave us. NOW!" he roared, and the cranky old man ran down the path.

When he reached the outskirts of his village, the man felt his face. He was disappointed when he felt the lump on the left side of his face was still there, but when he compared it to his right cheek, he found another, identical lump. He had both his own lump, and now his neighbor's lump on his face.

The new lump would not come off. It seemed as permanent as if it had been on his face since birth. As he realized what had hap-

pened, the old man fell to the ground, crying. All of the mean old man's meanness disappeared, leaving only sorrow.

The Man Who Brought the Dead Back to Life

Just yesterday I heard the most amazing story from an older servant talking with a younger servant apprenticed to his house. It was about Heibō! Remember? The boy from our town who disappeared so long ago? It went something like this:

You probably never heard about old Heibō, did you? He worked here a long time ago, long time ago. He just showed up at the master's doorstep one morning and said "Use me." He's a story waiting to be told, you know. Here, sit down and let me tell you about him.

He was straight from the fields and didn't know the first thing about living in the big city. But the master is a generous man, as you'll see when you've been here as long as I have. I told him about the kid and the master called to see him. Seeing that he was fit and able, and old enough for hard work, my master told him he would see what positions were available.

"Use you?" the master asked. "What can you do?"

"Anything."

"Anything?"

"Name it."

"Stoking the fires for the bath."

24

That would do it for most people. No one wants to stoke the fires in the bath. I've been a servant all my life and I can't think of any job I hate more than stoking the fires. It's hot and dirty, and it's really hard work keeping the fires fed and stoked. And the fire burns all the air so you find yourself gasping and choking while the fire burns out. Plus you have to keep the fire just right, so the baths are warm enough to please the master without giving him a good scald. Hell hath no fury like even a lightly boiled master.

Plus, it's a lot of responsibility to tend the fires. If they get away from you, the whole neighborhood will be up in smoke before you can say "tinderbox."

We rotated the job between able men on the master's staff, so that we could take turns doing it. Even so, no one was really happy with the situation. The master knew this, and was looking for someone to take the job full-time.

But the country kid was anxious to start his life in the city. "It just so happens that I am the best fire-stoker and bath-tender in these parts," he blurted. "I'll take the job."

He started that day, and it was obvious he didn't know the first thing about stoking a fire. But I was pretty happy to have somebody to keep the fires full time—it meant I didn't have to—so I showed him how to do everything and he caught the hang of it after a few days.

After a few days with no major mishaps, the master came down and told the kid the job was his to keep.

"What shall we call you," asked the master.

"I forgot."

Until this point the staff had been calling him "country boy," "fire boy," and things like that. No one knew his real name.

"You forgot," the master repeated. He wasn't sure if the boy was lying because he was in trouble with the authorities or if the kid was just playing with him. Or if he was really telling the truth. But, as I said before, the master is a generous man. "So we shall give you a new name. From this moment on you are to known as Heibō, 'Ash Boy'."

Heibō was a hard worker, and he came to be accepted as one of the staff. He was a pretty ordinary young man until New Year's.

On the second day of the New Year, Heibō came to breakfast and told us all he had had a wonderful dream. Of course, good dreams around New Year's are a sign of good fortune in the year to come, so we were all interested in Heibō's dream. But he wouldn't tell any of us what it was.

Eventually, news of Heibō's good dream got around to the master. The master was very interested, and thought that if one of his servants was going to have some good fortune, that luck should be spread out to include everyone in the master's household as well. He called for his fire-stoker and asked him to sit down.

"So, Heibō. Sell me your dream," my master said.

"Sell you my dream?"

"You heard me. What do you want for it?"

"I can't sell you my dream. It was a good one. It was more than a good one. It was wonderful, truly a good omen."

"Be reasonable. I am your master at this house. I want, I need the dream. Whatever you want for it is yours, but I must have it."

But Heibō refused. "There is no good reason to sell this dream. I wouldn't sell it for any amount of money," he told the master.

This went on for some time, with the master all but begging Heibō to sell his dream, and with Heibō refusing every time, no matter what wealth was offered.

The negotiations continued for several hours until the master suddenly collapsed. He was taken to his quarters and put to bed.

But the master's sudden illness did not give Heibō a moment's rest, for the master's daughter renewed the discussion where her father had left off. "My father has told you he wants your dream very badly. Because of you and your dream, the master of this house has taken ill. Even now he lies asleep, dreaming of having your dream. Why will you not sell him your dream? Has he been unfair with you?"

"He has been an excellent master," replied the

fire-stoker, tired from the day's events. "But this dream is so special I could never sell it."

Offer, refusal, offer, refusal, offer, refusal—Heibō and the master's daughter debated their cases late into the night until the two fell fast asleep.

The next morning the master's daughter awoke first.

"Heibō, get up," she said in a voice filled with fear.

The two ran down the stairs just to meet the master on his way up them. He was red with rage, and swung at Heibō, who jumped back up the stairs. "Heibō, you cur! As much as I offer you, you refuse to sell your dream to me at any price. But you find it in yourself to sleep with my daughter? You are the lowest of dogs."

The master's daughter burst into tears and tried to explain their innocence. But before she could explain, her maids grabbed her and took her to her room.

Two of the master's other servants grabbed Heibō and held him while a third tied him up. "You," said the master, "are to be exiled to the Isle of Demons!"

The servants contracted with a captain to deliver Heibō to the Isle of Demons. The ship set out at once, and arrived at the island after two days at sea. Still tied in his ropes, Heibō was tossed on the shore and left for dead.

Presently, a demon came along the shore, looking for food. Naturally, he was overjoyed to find a nice meaty human all tied up and waiting to be eaten. The demon was so happy he almost ate Heibō without even cooking him first. But he remembered his father, the demon leader of the Isle of Demons. "It wouldn't do to keep all this to myself," thought the demon as he poked Heibō in the ribs. "I should share him with my father."

So the demon threw Heibō across his back and returned to his father's palace. He unloaded his find and proudly told his father, "Look what I found for supper!"

"Hmm, indeed!" bellowed the demon chief. "Where did you find this? There's a lot of meat on him. What a great idea for dinner."

"He found me on the shore, where I was left

after my master exiled me to this island," Heibō
answered for the demon.

"Did he now?" asked the chief. "And why did
he do that?"

Heibō told the demon the story of the dream
he would not sell and then the trouble first with
the master's sickness, then with his problems
with the master's daughter.

The dream intrigued the demon chief, who
asked about it.

"I couldn't tell you about the dream," protested Heibō. "It is such a precious jewel. Telling you would be the worse than selling it to
you."

"What can I offer you for your dream?" the
demon asked.

"Money is no good. This dream is special,
not something that can be bought easily."

The human and the demon haggled and
haggled until the demon made an offer Heibō
could not refuse.

"What about some magical items? I have
here the Needle of Death, the Needle of Life,
and the Thousand *Ri* Staff."

"And?"

"And? These are some of the most powerful
items known to man. Used properly, these can
make you a great and wealthy man."

"Hmmm," said Heibō, less than impressed.

"The Needle of Death is most powerful.
With it, one stab to a foe's ear will dispatch him
to the world of the dead instantly.

"The Needle of Life works in the same way. If you use it on someone or something dead, it will bring them back to life. There are no nasty side-effects, either. It'll be as if they had only been sleeping.

"The Thousand *Ri* Staff is different. All you need to do is hold it and say 'Go a thousand *ri*,' and you will be transported that distance in the twinkling of an eye."

Heibō's eye lit up with the demon's explanations of the tools. "Those sound very impressive," he said. "I think we have a deal."

"Excellent, excellent," said the chief. "Now, give me the dream."

"The items first, please."

"As you wish," said the demon. He handed the human the needles and the staff. "Now, give me the dream."

The chief led Heibō into a large room where the two could talk without others listening in and stealing the dream. The chief sat upon a throne and beckoned Heibō closer. The human cupped his hand and leaned over to whisper in the chief's ear. But as the chief leaned toward him, Heibō pulled the Needle of Death from his pocket. He slipped it into the chief's ear and *sssssstt* the demon chief was dead.

Then Heibō leapt out a window into the demon chief's garden. Holding the Thousand *Ri* Staff, he gave the command, "A thousand *ri*." Instantly, he was transported a thousand *ri* away from the Island of Demons.

Heibō found himself on a grassy plain by a Buddhist temple. The sun was going down, so he decided to stay the night at the temple. No one seemed to be in the temple, so Heibō made himself at home and went to sleep. No sooner had he nodded off to sleep than he heard a great commotion. A group—a large group from the sound of them—had entered and was gathering in the main room.

"What a tragedy," wailed a woman. "What a horrible, horrible tragedy."

"She was only seventeen," added an old man's voice. "What a tragedy for the Rich Man of the East."

"A man as rich as he, and he couldn't buy his daughter's health. That shows what good money'll do you," said a third. "He would've done anything to save her, but she's gone just the same."

Heibō watched the group of townspeople through a space in the doors separating his room from the main room. They brought the girl's body into the temple and set it in the center of the room.

"Such a good family, such a beautiful girl, a wonderful child... to meet such an awful fate...."

"There is nothing for us to do now but pray," said another man.

The group began to recite a Buddhist chant.

"Aha," Heibō thought. "I will bring the daughter of the Rich Man of the East back to life with the Needle of Life."

The townspeople left the temple after a few hours of prayer. Heibō pulled the Needle of Life from his belt and stole from his room. The dead girl was as beautiful as the townspeople had said.

He leaned over her still body and pushed the Needle into her ear. The girl's eyes fluttered, and she looked very surprised to find herself in the village temple.

"What happened? Where am I? Oooh, my head hurts."

She was surprised when Heibō told her she had died, but she believed him when she saw she was wearing a funeral gown.

"My family must be grieving," she said. "I must go home and show them I am alive."

"No, wait until the morning. If you go at night, still in your funeral clothes, they may think you are a ghost."

So the two waited in the dark temple until the first light of morning crept into the temple.

Heibō waited at the temple while the girl returned home. The girl's four-year-old sister saw her first. *"Onee-chan* (big sister)*!"* she yelled with glee. *"Onee-chan!"*

A nursemaid laughed sadly, and told the child, "No, no. Your sister won't be coming back for a long—It *is* your big sister!"

The child ran to her sister and grabbed her hands. The nursemaid screamed and passed out. The young sister's happy noises drew the father's attention, and he looked out to see what the commotion was all about. When he saw his daughter, he too was surprised. He ran to the door of the home and embraced his daughter.

"But you were dead! Dead! How did you

come back?" He broke off the embrace and held her at arm's length. "How long can you stay? Will you have to go back to the land of the dead soon? Is this some sort of trick?"

"I *was* dead," said the girl. "But I was fortunate. The greatest doctor in all Japan was in the temple last night. He brought me back to life somehow."

"Where is this doctor? We must find him! Quickly, before he leaves us. I must show my thanks to this man."

Word that the dead daughter of the Rich Man of the East had been brought back to life spread quickly through the town. Over half the town's people joined the rich man and his daughter to greet the doctor at the temple.

"Thank for bringing my daughter back to me!" cried the happy father. "Thank you! You must visit my house for a celebration in your honor."

Heibō agreed readily, and a great feast was held at the home of the Rich Man of the East. The entire town joined the celebration. The townspeople thanked Heibō and made him an honorary citizen of their town. The Rich Man of the East was more generous, awarding Heibō no small amount of money. Then, later in the celebration, he offered Heibō his daughter.

"I must have you for my son-in-law. Please, marry my daughter, the daughter you saved. Live with me in comfort and luxury."

Heibō looked at his clothes, torn and tattered from work stoking the fire, torn further
still from his rough treatment at the Isle of Demons. "No, I cannot. I am the Man Who Brings
the Dead Back to Life. I mean no offense, but it
would not be proper for me to be anybody's son-
in-law just yet."

The Rich Man of the East pleaded with
Heibō late into the night, trying to win him for
his daughter. But Heibō's resolve was strong.
The rich man's daughter was beautiful, but
Heibō knew it was not time to marry just then.
He did, however, accept the rich man's offer to
stay in his house as a guest for several days.

The next morning Heibō was met with one
of those coincidences that only happens in songs
and fairy tales: when he awoke, he heard the
servants mention the daughter of the Rich Man
of the West had died suddenly during the night.
In another remarkable coincidence, the girl was
very beautiful, and had died at only seventeen.

Heibō was well known in the town for saving
the daughter of the Rich Man of the East, so he
was dressed and ready when a plea for his
"medical skills" reached his door. He went to
the home of the Rich Man of the West and asked
to be left alone with the girl's body. Out came
the Needle of Life, and the girl found herself
alive and awake again.

The Rich Man of the West, like the Rich
Man of the East had done before him, threw a

tremendous feast. And again, like the Rich Man of the East, the Rich Man of the West asked Heibō to marry his daughter.

When the Rich Man of the East heard of his rival's offer, he repeated the offer of *his* daughter's hand. The two rich men began to espouse the virtues of their daughters, each telling Heibō how only *his* was the perfect bride. Tempers soon flared, but before the two men came to blows Heibō coughed quietly.

All eyes turned to the Man Who Brings the Dead Back to Life. "I see that if I do not marry one of your daughters there will be no peace in this town." He paused briefly for dramatic effect. "And if I choose the daughter of the Rich Man of the East, those favoring the Rich Man of the West will split this town with jealousy. If I choose to marry the daughter of the Rich Man of

the West, those favoring the Rich Man of the East will destroy the town with rage."

He paused again, letting his words sink in. "I am in a quandary. The only way out of this crisis, the only way I can solve this great problem is... to marry both daughters. I will become a son-in-law to each of you."

The two rich man agreed that was the best solution. It was decided that Heibō would spend fifteen days as the son-in-law of the Rich Man of the East, then fifteen days as the son-in-law of the Rich Man of the West. Everyone was happy with the idea, even the two daughters.

The townspeople praised Heibō's wisdom as much as they praised the miracles he had performed bringing the dead girls back to life. Heibō was very gracious, and accepted this praise with a smile. But the real reason for the smile was the dream he had seen on the first night of the new year. Every detail of the dream had come true! That was why he couldn't sell his dream!

Kasa Jizō,
or Kindness Repaid

A LONG, long time ago there was an elderly couple living on the outskirts of town. They had lived a reasonably happy life together for a number of years. Where familiarity is thought to breed contempt in some relationships, their many years together only strengthened their love for each other. Together, they had lived through all sorts of hardships, and they were confident they could overcome any others that might come their way.

One winter day the old woman said to the old man, "I know we don't have enough money for anything extravagant, but it's almost *oshōgatsu*. It would be nice to have some pine to decorate the house, or some *miso* soup, or some *mochi*. What should we do this year?"

"Don't you worry about that. I've been saving a little something for a rainy day." The old man reached into a closet and pulled down a box of spun cotton. "I'll spin this into balls of yarn tonight. Tomorrow morning I'll get up and go sell them at the town market. I'll buy some rice for *mochi*, some pine and the other stuff for decorations and I'll be back before dark. If I get enough for the yarn I'll even get a little fish for our supper." And with that, the man set to work.

The next morning, the old man put a towel around his head for warmth, packed five freshly spun balls of yarn into his pack, and set out for the town. A light dusting of snow fell as the man started up the hills to town. Deep snow on the road made the going tediously slow. A bright sky greeted him as he crested a ridge, but off in the distance the old man saw a line of fierce, black clouds. "Another blizzard," he thought. "I hope it holds off until I make it home."

"Yarn! Homespun yarn here! Make a fine sweater with this homespun yarn!" The old man called on the townspeople to buy his yarn. The market was crowded with people doing their last-minute *oshōgatsu* shopping, but no one was interested in yarn. People wanted pine for decorations, rice for *mochi* and other seasonal things. No matter how well spun it was, no one wanted homespun yarn at this time of year.

"Homespun yarn! A fine present for the ladies! Cheap! It'll make fine clothes, don't you know! Sturdy and warm! Buy a ball of yarn!" The man called and called all day, but no one bought his yarn. The shoppers began to thin out late in the afternoon, and the old man realized it was time to give up.

He packed his yarn and worked his way through the crowd. Before he made it to the road, another merchant caught his eye and asked, "Giving up already?"

"It's been a long day and I haven't sold a thing."

"Same here," said the merchant. "I wanted to sell these bamboo hats to get some *oshōgatsu* goodies for the wife, but I've been here all day and no one's so much as looked in my direction."

"I know what you mean," said the old man. "They're all after rice and decorations for the new year. I don't blame them, but I can't go home empty-handed."

The other trader thought a moment, then said, "Here, let's do this: How 'bout I give you these five hats—all brand new, mind you, and made from the best bamboo in these parts—and you give me your five balls of homespun?"

The two agreed that a trade was a little better than going home completely empty-handed, so they exchanged goods. Both men packed their bags and set out for their homes.

Dark clouds rolled over the town just as he left. He looked at the swollen snow-clouds and wondered if he would make it home before the worst of the storm hit.

He did not. The snow picked up intensity quickly, growing from a powder-like dusting to a driving blizzard in the blink of an eye. The old man tried his best to hurry along the hilly trails, but somewhere along the way he got lost. Rather than wander around lost in a blizzard, the man looked for somewhere to stop and rest.

He rounded a bend in the trail and found a small roadside shrine. It was a typical roadside shrine, with a few devotional statues of carved stone along a road to keep travelers safe during their journey. The statues were uncovered, and snow had fallen on them—six statues in all— giving them the appearance of six snowmen lined up along the road.

"You must be cold," the man spoke to the statues. "You should have a proper roof over your heads, you know. This is miserable enough weather for men, but for you..."

The man was no more superstitious than the next person, but he believed everything had its place in the world. The statues were there to protect travelers, and now, at *oshōgatsu*, his heart was moved to do a good turn for them in return. He pulled a rag from his pack and brushed the snow from each statue. Then, real-izing that without some sort of protection from the elements the snow would only bury them again, the old man took the hats from his pack.

"Someone should be taking better care of you fellows. I was taking these home to my wife, but you need them more than I do." He put a hat on each statue, then tied the cord around each statue's head. But he only had five hats. When he reached the sixth, he took off the towel covering his own head and tied it around the last statue.

"There," he said to the statues. "Happy New

Year, fellows, and take care. I've got to get home."

Bare-headed and with an empty pack, the man set out to find his way home. He walked and walked, trudging through the snow for what seemed like hours. After some time the road fell away to a path again. The path criss-crossed with other trails, and eventually the old man found the trail that led to his home.

"*Tadaima*, I'm home," he said, and threw his pack on the floor.

His wife came to greet him. "*Okaeri nasai*, welcome home." Then, seeing his pack was empty, she asked, "The yarn sold well?"

It was against the man's nature to lie, especially to his wife, so he took a deep breath and began to tell his story. When he had finished, he waited silently for her appraisal of the situation. He was afraid she would be angry with him—or worse, diasppointed. But his wife greeted him with praise. "What a nice thing to do! We're at an age where we really don't need *oshōgatsu* and things like that anyway. Come on and warm yourself by the fire. I'll get you something warm to drink."

The couple ate their new year's eve dinner of rice gruel and hot water in a festive spirit, then went to bed. The blizzard continued pouring snow down upon their house, and a fierce winter wind howled. But the couple's home was warm and cozy. The two quickly drifted off to sleep.

Sometime in the dead of night the two woke with a start. "I had a horrible dream," said the man. "People were chasing me, calling my name."

His wife stared at him in the inky darkness. "I had the same dream!"

Before they could say another word they heard a strange sound. At first it sounded like the wind wailing and howling, but soon they heard what seemed like voices chanting. After a few moments the chant became clear.

> *Where is the home of the kind old man and*
> *Where is the home of the old man's wife?*
> *Where is the home of the kind old man and*
> *Where is the home of the old man's wife?*

The couple jumped up and ran to the door, whereupon the chant changed.

> *Is this the home of the kind old man and*
> *Is this the home of the old man's wife?*
> *Is this the home of the kind old man and*
> *Is this the home of the old man's wife?*
> *Hoi sa hoi sa hoi hoi hoi*
> *Yoi sa yoi sa yoi yoi yoi*

The voices were quite close, but they had not found the house. They changed their chant once more.

> *We are the statues the old man sheltered.*
> *We want to find the kind old man.*
> *Where is the home of the kind old man and*
> *Where is the home of the old man's wife?*

The old man opened the door and yelled in a voice loud enough to be heard over the raging winds:

> *I am the old man you met on the highway.*
> *This is my house and this is my wife.*

Then he shut the door and held it fast, afraid of what might happen next.

The storm died down suddenly, and the winds became still. Through the door the old couple heard the *shuuka-shuuka-shuuka* of people marching through the snow. The sound stopped.

Then they heard a great noise. THUNK-SHHHPPPEEEWWWW!!! They held the door with all their might, but nothing pushed against it.

Then they heard the *shuuka-shuuka-shuuka* sound again, this time fading off into the distance. They opened the door a tiny bit to see what was out there. A large sack was sitting just outside the door, and nothing else. No statues, no people, nothing else. The man told his wife to stay inside. He went to the sack and pushed it with his foot, but he could not tell what it might contain. Working up his courage, the man looked into the sack and saw—*mochi*, pine and new year's decorations—and gold! The bag held a fortune in gold! He called to his wife, and as she stood by his side in the eerily quiet night, marveling at the bag of treasure, the two heard distant voices chant.

This is your reward
For sharing your kindness
Thank you again
For sharing your gift.
This is your reward
For sharing your kindness
Thank you again
For sharing your gift.

Off in the distance they could just see six shapes marching away down the path. Five wore bamboo hats: the leader wore the old man's towel on his head.

Momotarō, the Peach Boy

Long, long ago in a remote part of Japan lived a very unhappy old man and his wife. The couple was very poor, and had to work hard every day just to put the day's food on the table. Despite his age, the old man worked from dawn to dusk as a laborer on nearby farms. While he was away cutting wild grass and trees to clear space for fields, his wife was home tending their own small field, washing clothes and making constant repairs to the tiny hut they called home.

The source of the old couple's unhappiness was not their poverty or their hard life, nor did it lie with a lack of love in their life together. The one thing that weighed down their hearts and haunted their dreams was that they had no children.

One morning much like any other the couple rose and started out for work. The man took up his tools and set out for a nearby farm, while the woman loaded the day's laundry into a tub and headed down to the river.

When the woman reached the river she took out their tattered old clothes and started to wash. She did the work mechanically, without thinking. This left her mind free to ponder what evil she and the old man could have done to offend the gods enough to warrant the punishment of a life without children.

Reaching for another shirt, she saw to her surprise a great ball floating slowly down the river toward her. As it came closer, she saw that this ball was a huge peach, almost three feet around.

"I have never seen such a peach, such a huge, huge peach," she said aloud. "It must surely be sweet and ripe and ready to eat. Wouldn't it make a nice supper for us tonight!"

But the river was wide and there were no branches or sticks the woman could use to pull in the great peach. Frightened at the thought that such a great peach would slip through her grasp, she suddenly found herself repeating an old verse she had learned as a child. She had no idea why the long-forgotten verse suddenly emerged from her memory, but the words came out with a tune so beautiful she didn't believe the voice was hers as she sang:

> *The far waters are bitter,*
> *The near waters are sweet.*
> *Pass through the bitter,*
> *And come to the sweet.*

As the old woman repeated the verse, the peach began to bob toward her side of the river. Slowly at first, the peach crossed against the current and floated to where the old woman could reach out and, still singing, grab it in her arms.

"Such a fine peach," though the woman as she examined it. "What a nice surprise for the old man's dinner!"

The great peach was so large she could hardly hold it in her arms, so she put it in the laundry basket, piled her laundry on top of it and hurried home with the prize.

The old man came home just after sunset. His back was sore and his arms were tired from the day's work.

The old woman ran out to meet him. "At last you're home," she said. "I've been waiting all day! Hurry, come in, come in."

"What's the matter? Is something wrong? What happened? Is everything all right?" The old man was alarmed—the old woman was not usually this excited.

"Nothing's wrong, but I have a nice present for you. Hurry, come see it!"

"Ah," said the weary old man. He bent over and washed his feet, which were dirty from the road home, then entered the hut.

"Look! Just look at this!" said the old woman.

The old man was taken aback for a moment. Confused at what appeared to be a huge peach in his hut, he asked "A peach? Is this a peach?" he asked. Then the confusion turned to a rare show of irritation. "A peach? How could you buy such a peach when you yourself know how little money we have?"

"But I did not buy it," the woman answered. "I found it at the river this morning." And the woman told the story of how she found the peach.

The old man listened to the tale, he said "We should not spurn this gift from the heavens. I am hungry—let's eat it." He took the kitchen knife and turned the peach around, looking for the best place to cut.

Just as the old man was about to make the cut, the peach suddenly split itself in half, revealing a beautiful young boy in place of a pit.

"Wait a minute, old man!" said the boy.

The old man dropped the knife in surprise and bowed his head in reverence of the beautiful boy within the most unusual peach.

"Rise! Don't be afraid," said the boy. "I am not a demon here to haunt you. I am a gift from

the heavens. Your sorrow has not been over-looked, and I have been sent to you as your son."

The old man looked at the old woman in disbelief, and she at him. Then they hugged each other, tears of joy rolling down their cheeks. The old woman picked up the child and hugged him. Then the old man did the same.

"Do you have a name?" asked the old man.

"You are my parents. Do not parents name their children themselves?" replied the child.

"Then your name shall be Momotarō, the peach boy."

The years passed quickly and Momotarō grew into a tall, strong young man. He was a hard worker, known in the town below the old couple's farm for his courage and cleverness, and for his kind heart.

When he was fifteen, Momotarō sat down to talk with his father. "You have been very good to me. You have shown me love and kindness greater than the mountains are high and the rivers are deep, and I am most grateful."

Momotarō's way of speaking was very stiff and formal, and the old man was a bit surprised. "Of course we have shown you kindness," he said. "You are our son. We love you. It's only natural that we should take care of you. And when we get a little older we will be unable to work. Then you will take care of us."

He paused and asked, "Why do you speak to your father so formally now?"

"Because," Momotarō began, "I don't want to seem ungrateful or selfish in any way, but I have a favor to ask of you."

"Of course," said the old man, "anything I can give you is yours. Just ask."

"I must ask to leave you for some time," said the youth.

The old man was surprised by this. "But, why? Have we not given you everything possible? Have we not loved you, my son? Are you dissatisfied with your life with us?"

"No, no. Nothing of the sort. It is difficult to explain, my father. I will return to take care of you and my mother before long, but I must leave you."

"But, where will you go?" asked the old man.

"Far from here is an island of devils and demons," explained Momotarō. "These demons often come here, to Japan, killing and eating innocent people, stealing their belongings and destroying whatever they can't take with them. I am going to end their reign of terror."

The old man sat back and scratched his chin. "I know you are no ordinary boy," he told his son. "You are a child of the heavens, and you no doubt have a great mission ahead of you. You are strong and tall, you know no fear and you are both smart and compassionate without equal. Truly, if this island of great evil exists, you are the one to destroy it."

"Then I may go?" asked Momotarō.

"I cannot stop you. I ask only that you hurry

back to your mother and father when your
struggle is over."

The old couple spent that night pounding
rice into cakes for Momotarō to take on his journey. There were tears in their eyes the next
morning as they said good-bye to their son, but
they knew somehow that theirs was no ordinary
child. He would return victorious.

Momotarō the warrior set out at a pace
faster than any normal man could walk. About
midday he sat down for lunch and a short nap
under a tree in a large field of high grasses. He
had just opened his pouch of rice cakes when a
dog as large as a small horse came charging out
of the grass at him.

"You dare to cross my fields without my permission?" snarled the huge dog. "I should kill
you where you sit, but I am compassionate.
Give me all your rice cakes and I will let you
leave with your life. Otherwise, your life will be
mine."

Momotarō gave the great dog a cold stare
and said with a mocking laugh, "You are the
daring one, dog. I am Momotarō. I am on my
way to the island of great evil, where I will kill
the devils that eat our people and rob and plun-
der our land. If you stand in my way, I will cut
you in half, lengthwise. Slowly."

At once, the dog dropped his tail between his
legs and fell to the ground, groveling.

"You are Momotarō? I mean, you are **the** Momotarō? I have been disrespectful to the Momotarō famous for his courage and strength?" asked the dog as humbly and politely as possible.

And thinking of his own safety, the dog added, "And compassion? Famous for his great compassion? You are going to the Island of Evil to kill the devils? I would consider it an honor, a tremendous honor, if a rude dog such as myself could accompany the great Momotarō on his mission to slaughter the demons."

"I think I could take you," said Momotarō, and the warrior opened his pouch for a rice cake.

"I am very hungry," said the dog. "Could I humbly ask for one of your rice cakes?"

"These? These are the best rice cakes in the land," said Momotarō. "I couldn't possibly part with a whole one, but if you like, I'll give you half of one."

The pair ate their lunch quickly, then set out for the island of devils.

Momotarō and the giant dog continued on through a forest, whereupon a creature came down from the trees and stood in the middle of the path. As Momotarō drew closer, he saw it was a large monkey.

"Greetings. You are Momotarō, are you not? You are off to battle?" asked the monkey.

Momotarō nodded.

"You are welcome in my part of the country," said the monkey. "May I have the privilege of accompanying..."

"You'll do nothing of the sort," snarled the dog. "Get out of the way before we kill you. We're off to kill the demons and devils on the Island of Evil." The jealousy in the dog's voice bared itself as he growled, "What can a monkey do in battle that a dog cannot do better? We have no need for your sort—away with you!"

The monkey turned to the dog and said, "I addressed the great Momotarō, not his pet."

With that, the two giant animals closed on each other, snarling, with fangs bared and claws outstretched.

Here it stands to be noted that dogs and monkeys hate each other, and will fight at al-

most any opportunity. In addition to this in-
stinctive animosity, the giant dog was afraid
the addition of the monkey would lower his own
importance.

But before either animal could attack,
Momotarō stepped between them. "What's the
problem, dog? Don't you think anyone brave
enough to challenge the demons with us de-
serves our respect for his bravery?"

The dog stopped growling, but kept his
fangs bared.

Momotarō then turned to the monkey.
"Who are you, and do you really wish to join us?"

"I am just a hill monkey. Word of your expedition to the island of the devils traveled like
lightening. When I heard of it, I wanted to find
you and join you."

"You are welcome, brave hill monkey. Come
with us."

Although Momotarō strictly warned the
monkey and dog not to quarrel, they would
snarl and scratch at each other the moment the
warrior's back was turned. This division in the
ranks caused Momotarō no end of irritation,
and he finally decided to separate the two.

He gave his pennant to the dog and sent him
ahead as his standard-bearer. Next, he gave his
sword to the monkey and sent him to follow behind. In this way, Momotarō kept the enemies
separated, yet with equally honorable positions
in the expedition.

Thus separated, the three set out again for the island of devils and demons.

After some time, the party came upon a field, and in the field, a pheasant. The pheasant was the most beautiful bird Momotarō had seen, with colorful feathers in a handsome design. The dog, in the lead, saw only a hindrance and perhaps a meal, and he charged the bird.

But the bird was quick, and flew over the dog, then swooped back to nip the beast in the tail. The dog turned, then jumped high in the air, just missing the bird. The bird countered, diving swiftly at the dog and missing only by a matter of inches. The battle went on for some time. The bird made a number of quick attacks which the dog cleverly evaded, and the dog attacked repeatedly with all its strength only to watch the bird avoid his long fangs by the slimmest of margins.

Momotarō watched the fight with amusement. Clearly, the bird was an excellent fighter. But the battle was wasting precious time and delaying his journey. The warrior stepped up and restrained the dog.

"You are delaying us, bird. Move aside or fight the three of us," said Momotarō.

The bird hovered for a moment, then looked at the pennant the dog had set aside. He recognized the pennant as that of the great Momotarō and turned pale with the realization. All color drained from his beautiful plumage and he landed, bowing deeply before the dog and his leader.

"I must apologize, Momotarō," the bird stuttered. "How was I to know the dog attacking me was one of your servants? I apologize most humbly, most humbly."

The dog bared his teeth and moved toward the prostrate bird. But Momotarō held the dog back, saying, "You are a fine and courageous fighter bird. Accompany us and you may live. Otherwise..."

"It would be an honor, Momotarō," said the pheasant.

"But Momotarō," whined the dog, "this bird has attacked your procession. And what good is a bird in combat against demons and devils? Can you seriously mean to allow this bird to join our party?"

The monkey, who had by this time caught up with the rest of the party, said, "As disagreeable to me as it is, I must agree with the dog. What good is a bird to us? We appreciate your compassion, but please think of the battle ahead."

Long irritated by the bickering between the two beasts, Momotarō was angry with them. "I am Momotarō, the leader of this expedition to fight the evils that threaten our land. You will obey my commands or you will answer to me. Should you care to part company with me, I am not afraid to fight the demons by myself."

He added a dramatic pause, then asked, "Is this understood?"

The monkey and the dog silently stared at the ground.

"Good. How do you expect to fight demons and devils when you are so intent on attacking one another? From this day onward the three of you will be the best of friends. If you dare to fight or argue, you will answer to me on the spot."

And with that, the party of four silently set out again for the land of the devils.

The four traveled through a number of hardships, strictly heeding Momotarō's edict against quarreling. In the course of their travels the three animals overcame their dislike for one another and eventually became friendly, if not close.

Each animal proved his merits before the others, and each recognized the strengths the other possessed. The dog's power and strength impressed the others, but he saw in turn the speed and flying skill of the bird and the resourcefulness and climbing skills of the monkey.

At last, the party left the forest and came upon some cliffs that overlooked the sea. It was the first time the animals had seen the sea, and all three were awestruck by its seemingly endless expanse that rolled out before them.

"Ah, Momotarō. About the sea... it's so, so... big," said the dog.

"I could never fly all the way to the demons' island. How will we get there?" said the pheasant.

"But there are no trees anywhere to be seen. What can I do?" asked the monkey.

Momotarō had sensed their fear even before they had spoken. He responded harshly. "After all our trials you are afraid of the sea? Well, you are weak. I should have recognized this from the start."

"You are free to go on your way. You wouldn't be of any worth in battle anyway. Away with you, all of you! Out of my sight!"

"But Momotarō," spoke the pheasant, "we've come so far for this."

"Yes," added the dog. "We can't turn back now. What would we do?"

"You must let us continue, we must reach the Island of Evil," said the monkey.

"We're not afraid of the sea," said the pheasant.

"Not at all," said the dog.

"No, not at all. Not in the slightest," added the monkey.

"You must take us with you," they said in unison.

Hearing this, Momotarō smiled and said, "Very well. Let us be off."

The party found a small port city and met with the mayor. On hearing the famous Momotarō was on his way to fight the demons, the mayor quickly offered the party the best ship in the town for the journey. However, the mayor politely declined Momotarō's suggestion that he join the party.

"Someone," said the mayor slowly, "has to take care of the town and townspeople while you are away."

The sea journey took some time, but eventually the monkey, keeping watch from high upon the ship's mast, called down to the others.

"Land! I see land dead ahead!"

As the ship neared the island, Momotarō and his companions knew they had found the Island of Evil. From the island's blackened, burnt-out landscape to the long jagged edges of the castle on the hill, the entire island seemed to radiate evil.

"We've come this far," thought Momotarō

to himself. "How should we defeat the evil?"

After some thought, the warrior called for the pheasant.

"Bird," ordered Momotarō. "You have flight and speed. Fly ahead and make the first assault on the demons. We will follow right behind you."

The pheasant was happy to have the honor of leading the attack, and flew off at once. When he reached the castle, he first flew around the demons to disturb them and attract their attention.

The first demon the pheasant saw was as the legends had described—huge and hairy, with horns growing from his forehead. The other demons were about the same in appearance, though the colors of their skin and hair varied from dark red to dark stone gray.

The pheasant then perched on a high place in the castle and spoke so all could hear:

"Greetings, demons and dwellers in filth and scum. Greetings cannibals and murderers, thieves and robbers, rogues and scoundrels and whatever base form of man that accompanies you. I bear you greetings from Momotarō, warrior of the far land you so regularly pillage and abuse."

The demons gathered around the tower to watch this brilliantly colored bird speak.

"To be blunt," continued the pheasant, "Momotarō has come to kill you, and return the riches you have stolen to their rightful place. But Momotarō is not without compassion. If you wish to save your wretched little lives, you will surrender at once and return that which you have stolen."

The demons were still and silent.

"And break off your horns as a token of respect for our power," the pheasant went on. "If not, the four of us shall surely kill you all."

"The what?" grumbled an older looking demon. "The how many of you?"

"Momotarō the warrior, and his servants the dog, the hill monkey and myself," replied the bird.

At this, the demons laughed a chilling laugh and joked with one another. "Ooooh! Momotarō the big man and his traveling circus have come to slay us all!" said one.

"A pheasant! I'm so frightened! Someone

help me, save me from the terrible pheasant," laughed another in mock seriousness.

"It could be worse," joked another. "It could be a pigeon."

The demons were enjoying themselves a great deal when they remembered the pheasant. The demon closest to the bird slowly raised his terrible iron mace, hoping his move would go unnoticed. But the bird took to the air an instant before the great mace dropped, and the demon instead struck the wall on which the pheasant had been perched.

The bird took advantage of this, using his talons to scratch at the eyes of the demon. The demon, in great pain, swung the mace wildly and hit another nearby demon by mistake.

The bird then flew quickly from demon to demon, scratching and spitting so fiercely the demons swore they were fighting a whole army of birds. The bird would hover over a demon and scratch at his face until another demon came to rescue the first. Then the bird would move to another demon, and as often as not, the demon that had come to rescue his comrade would strike him by mistake.

As the pheasant delivered his warning, Momotarō and the others had docked the ship in a small cove and started for the castle on foot.

The demons were concentrating on the birds words, then on the birds attacks, so the other three could come right up to the gate unopposed. But the gate was formidable and strong, with great iron gates and fences studded with razor-sharp blades.

"Even the hill monkey, with his tree climbing expertise, would have a hard time with these walls," thought the warrior. As Momotarō looked at the castle walls he knew the next challenge would be finding a way to enter the fortress.

He and his two companions began a march around the castle in hopes of finding a weak spot somewhere, and as they walked they came to a stream. The stream ran through the castle and provided it with water, and Momotarō quickly realized this was a way into the fortress.

He followed the stream to the point where it flowed into the castle. Then he entered the water, which was shallow, and crawled under the walls. The monkey followed the warrior immediately, but the dog, who hated water, required a bit of coaxing from the other two before he joined them.

The bird had distracted the guards who would normally watch over the stream, so the three entered unnoticed. They quickly made their way to the pheasant, where they found themselves behind the demons, and they joined the battle at once.

The demons were surprised at finding an enemy behind them, but continued to fight. At first, the battle was even, but as Momotarō

killed demon after demon, his companions grew
bolder and the demons became more frightened.

Momotarō, his sword shining in the sun-
light, cut a path through the demons as his father cut grass from the fields. The pheasant
clawed with his talons and blinded demons with
the beating of his great wings. The dog charged
headlong into a demon and knock him to the
ground, then he tore at his throat viciously with
his powerful fangs. When the demons were
close enough, the monkey attacked with his
claws and teeth. When the enemy were further
away, the monkey threw stones and spears with
devastating accuracy. Together the four fought
as an army, and the demons soon broke ranks
and fled in every direction.

Some made for the castle walls, jumping
into the sea to meet a watery fate. Others tried

to hide in the castle itself, but the Momotarō soon found them and either put them to the sword or chased them over the walls.

Eventually only the king of the demons remained alive. As he looked over his castle, with his armies scattered and destroyed, he knew he was beaten. He did not run as Momotarō approached. He put down his mace and bowed a deep bow of humility. Then, he reached up and broke off his horns.

"I will honor my word," said Momotarō. "As you have torn your horns from your head, you will live. But I cannot let you, the leader of this great evil, free to roam the world. You are my prisoner, and you will return with me to the land you have so often abused."

The monkey tied the demons hands, then tied him firmly to the main gate of the castle. The four victorious warriors then searched the castle, freeing the countless prisoners the demons had kidnapped from Momotarō's homeland. They discovered the demons' great vaults of treasure, where they found riches beyond their imagination and great magical items and artifacts.

When they had loaded their bounty and the former prisoners on their ship, Momotarō brought the demon king on board. He told the monkey and dog to set the castle ablaze. With the castle burning in the distance, Momotarō gave the order to set sail for home.

Momotarō and his three comrades received

a hero's welcome when at last they reached
their port. There they divided the bounty and
started out on their way home.

One by one, the pheasant, the monkey and
the dog parted ways with Momotarō, each
pledging their loyalty to Momotarō and agree-
ing to meet again in the future.

Word of Momotarō's return reached his
hometown days before he did, and the whole
town celebrated with a great festival held in his
honor. But the happiest people in the town
were the old man and old woman who had
raised him from a child.

With tears in their eyes, they welcomed
their son home. Momotarō was also overjoyed
to be with his parents again.

"I have returned, as I promised," he told
them. "With the demons vanquished, you can

live the rest of your lives in safety. With the
demons' bounty, you can live the rest of your
lives in wealth and luxury."

And they did. Their descendants still have
the gratitude of people who remember how the
great Momotarō, the peach-boy, slew the demons and saved them all from the great evil.

Kintarō, the Young Atlas

Her husband had held a high government post in the court at Kyoto. He was not an evil man, but he had fallen prey to the petty politics of the court. He was stripped of his office on some pretense—his enemies' intrigue, no doubt—and he died soon after.

She knew that without him to protect her she had no chance to defend herself against these same enemies, so she fled to the mountains and began a new life alone. But not as alone as she might have thought, for soon after her husband's death she discovered she was pregnant with his child.

Thus, a child was born in the darkest depths of the deepest forests of Japan. For his mother, the child was the only good thing to have come from the past few years, the only light in a great sea of darkness. Appropriately, she named the child Kintarō, or Golden Boy.

The mother knew right away that her Kintarō was no ordinary child. Maybe it was the clean mountain water, or maybe it was the worry-free atmosphere of the countryside or the charm of the wilderness. Whatever it was, Kintarō was endowed with incredible physical strength.

His hobbies revealed this strength. At the age of seven he took great pleasure in lifting huge boulders and smashing them together to make gravel. He had tired of this by the age of eight, and he turned to cutting wood to pass his time. At that age he could fell the largest trees in better than half the time it took the most rugged woodsmen.

In time, Kintarō became well known to the few woodsmen that regularly passed through the mountains cutting down trees for lumber. They knew they were no match for the lad's strength, so rather than compete with him in a tree cutting contest or some other manly show of strength, they befriended him and taught him the ways of the woods.

The woodsmen were hardly the child's only friends. As the boy spent much of his time in the woods, he came to know the various animals of the forest. In time, he came to understand their languages, and he learned to speak with them in kind. Like the woodsmen, the animals of the forest respected young Kintarō, and treated him with warmth and respect. Also like the woodsmen, the animals taught him what they knew of the woods.

Of these animals, Kintarō was especially fond of the rabbits, deer, bears and monkeys. As he grew older, Kintarō spent more time wandering through the forest, gathering wood for his mother, bringing home food and doing other chores. In his wanderings he met his animal friends almost daily.

The bear was a wrestling partner, and the deer let Kintarō ride upon his back. The monkey taught him tree-climbing, while the hare was always a good sprinting partner.

One day when Kintarō was wandering the forest with his four animal friends, they came upon a treeless hill. The top of the hill was flat. The perfect place, the young Atlas decided, for a wrestling match.

"Let's play sumo," he said.

The others agreed and set about constructing a proper platform.

When they had finished, Kintarō announced, "Each of you will wrestle here, and I have a special prize for the winner of each bout."

"That sounds like fun," rumbled the bear confidently. "What is the prize?"

"You must wait until you—or someone else—wins," replied Kintarō.

"But what will you do?" asked the rabbit.

"I am a spectator," said Kintarō. "I will watch your bouts and judge them accordingly."

"Is that fair?" asked the deer.

"That's for you to decide," answered Kintarō "You're the umpire for the first bout."

"I am?"

"Yes," replied the youth. "The bout between monkey and rabbit."

"Oh, good! Yes, I will be the umpire!" answered the deer happily. "Rabbit, you start from over there, and Monkey, you will start on this side of the ring."

"Are you ready?" asked the umpire.

"You're in for it now, flop-ears," teased the monkey, to which the rabbit replied, "It won't take me long to finish with you, monkey boy."

"Now, now, let's be good sports," said the umpire as he stepped between the two wrestlers. "Ready? Go!"

The deer called the bout as a real sumo judge might, giving each wrestler warnings and progress reports as the bout went on, and offering encouragement to both sides.

"You're almost out of the ring there, rabbit. Take the offensive a little more. Show us some strength."

And when the rabbit gained an advantage, the deer would cheer, "Be careful, monkey. You know what he can do with his speed. Let him beat himself."

The bout was evenly pitched, with both contestants trying harder than usual to win before of an audience of friends.

Finally, the rabbit put the monkey on the defensive. The monkey gave ground, and as he retreated, he lost his balance a bit. The rabbit seized the moment and charged his opponent, knocking him out of the ring and onto his back in defeat.

"Ow! That hurt! Ooooh, my back hurts," cried the monkey, red with embarrassment and anger.

The deer looked to see that the monkey was uninjured, then proclaimed, "The bout is over. Rabbit wins his first match."

Kintarō reached into his pack and found the lunch his mother had prepared for him. He pulled out a rice dumpling and presented it to the winner. "Well done, rabbit. Well done."

Seeing the tasty prize for the winner, the monkey lost his temper and protested. "That wasn't fair! He didn't beat me! I fell when I lost my balance! I demand a rematch!"

Kintarō, the umpire and the bear discussed the matter and decided to grant the monkey his request. Rabbit, however, was allowed to keep his rice-dumpling.

The monkey was determined to win the rematch, and set his cunning monkey mind to beat the rabbit at any cost.

To this end, the monkey began the rematch by taking the rabbit's long ears and yanking them. The pain took rabbit by surprise, and the monkey easily pulled one of rabbit's legs out from under him.

This time the monkey was the victor, and Kintarō awarded monkey a rice-dumpling of his own.

"Would you mind a bout with me?" the deer asked the rabbit, who agreed readily. The bear rose and lumbered to the ring as umpire.

This match also went on for some time, but the rabbit finally found an advantage and brought the deer to his knees.

The contests went on and on to the merriment of all until finally all the players were tired.

"Enough for today," said Kintarō. "We can play more tomorrow. Let's go home."

The others, tired from their rough-housing, agreed and followed Kintarō down the hill to the valley that led to his home.

As they reached the bottom of the valley they found the stream there was much higher than normal. The ford was too deep to cross, and the animals were at a loss as to what to do.

Kintarō took charge, and told the animals, "Don't worry friends. I'll will get you across safely."

The boy then walked up and down the stream, looking at one tree, then another, shaking his head all the while.

Finally, he found the right tree, a monster tree so tall the animals could not see how high into the sky it stretched. He pushed and pushed and pushed with all his strength until the tree began to groan. Then it gave way with a crash and splashed into the water, spanning the swollen stream.

But the tree was not sturdy enough to use for a bridge, so Kintarō picked up several huge boulders, each several times heavier than the bear, and threw them into the stream so that they supported and strengthened his bridge.

The animals stood there with their mouths open, watching the wonder child. They had long known of Kintarō's great strength, but his power never failed to amaze them.

"Let's go," he said. "It's safe. Follow me."

As the animals and their companion crossed and disappeared on the other side of the stream, a woodsman emerged from a hiding place by the stream. He was in awe of the boy, and rushed to the stream to examine the bridge.

"What strength! What power!" he said, still amazed. "And he is only a boy? Who is that child? I must know."

The woodsman followed Kintarō and his companions until they went their separate ways and the boy returned to his home.

"Kin-chan! Where have you been?" asked his mother. "It's late. I was beginning to worry."

"We found a clearing in the woods and had a sumo tournament!" the youth said proudly.

"Who is 'we'?" the mother asked her son.

"The bear, the deer, the monkey and the rabbit."

"And who won?"

"Naturally, I would have, but I didn't join the tournament. I only watched and cheered." He didn't mention how he had shared the lunch his mother had made.

"Naturally," his mother mocked him. "You are a strong boy, but you should learn a little modesty. Who won the tournament?"

"Bear is the strongest of the group," said the boy. "After him it's hard to tell. Deer, rabbit and monkey are all pretty tough competitors."

Suddenly, the door to the cottage burst open and in walked the woodsman who had followed Kintarō from the stream. "Let's see how I'd do, little man," his deep voice filled the tiny cottage. "I'd like to join your next little tournament, if you wouldn't mind."

Kintarō was surprised and grabbed a club to defend his mother. "Who are you?" he demanded.

The stranger was not frightened by the club. "That doesn't matter so much now, does it?" he said. "If you're as strong as you think you are, how about a little arm-wrestling? Or aren't you feeling up to a challenge?"

Sure of himself, Kintarō warned the rude stranger. "If it is arm-wrestling you want, arm-wrestling you shall have. But you shouldn't be too disappointed if beat you."

"Oh, I won't, young lad, I won't."

The two set to arm-wrestling, with Kintarō's mother judging the contest. The two started evenly, and continued until Kintarō gained a small advantage. But no sooner had he done so than the woodsman turned the tables on him and Kintarō was on the defensive. The battle see-sawed for what seemed like hours until finally the challenger told the boy it was time to stop.

"It's a draw," he said. "I'm impressed, young man. I've met few men who could equal my

strength in arm-wrestling, and none that could best me. You are a most impressive child."

Kintarō was also silent. In truth, he was a bit surprised himself, for he had never before failed to win a contest of strength.

"I saw you at the stream this afternoon and I couldn't believe my own eyes," continued the woodsman. "Now I have tested your strength with my own, and I know you are truly something special. In a few years, when you are older, you may be the strongest man in all Japan."

The woodsman rose and turned to Kintarō's mother. "The boy is truly exceptional, amazing. Why is he here, in the middle of the woods? Why isn't he in the capital learning the samurai way? With his strength he would surely be an exceptional warrior."

"At one time I hoped my son would wear the two swords of the samurai," the mother began. "But he is as wild as the woods, uneducated and uncultured.

"His strength made him a very dangerous child. What if he killed a playmate in a wrestling match? I knew he would have some chance of becoming a samurai if we lived in the city, but the risks were too great.

"Besides, you can see for yourself that we are a poor family. I have no influence to introduce little Kin-chan to the right people. No, long ago I realized my dreams would never come true."

The woodcutter stood up and walked to a window of the small cottage. With his back to her, he said, "Perhaps I can help you."

Here young Kintarō showed his lack of culture. "You, a woodcutter? Will you introduce me to the king of the woodcutters?" he snorted.

The woodsman ignored the insult, and kept his gaze fixed on some point far outside the cottage.

"I am no woodcutter, boy, and in different times under different circumstances you might die for your insolence. But given the situation at hand, you will live."

The woodsman turned slowly, and continued, "I am Sadamitsu, general of Raikō, of the Minamoto."

He paused to let the words sink in, for Sadamitsu was a hero known and loved—or hated— throughout the country. Tales of his bravery and cunning as a general were eclipsed only by stories of his liege, Raikō.

"I am in disguise while I scour the countryside for young men worthy of joining my army, and it has been my happy surprise to find your son here, who is indeed an exceptional lad.

"With your permission, I would like to present Kintarō to Lord Raikō, to serve as a warrior."

"I have no doubt he will make an excellent samurai," he said, turning to Kintarō, "if he keeps his rude little mouth shut."

Kintarō's cheeks burned red as Sadamitsu's words stung home. He looked to his mother. Her expressionless face slowly grew into a small smile, then blossomed into a tremendous flower of happiness and gratitude that her dream might somehow come true. Her son might become a samurai.

"Yes," she beamed, "make him a samurai! Teach him the ways of the warrior! Please!"

"Excellent," said the general. "We should leave at once."

Kintarō's mother was surprised at the speed at which events had unfolded, and realized that though she was happy her son would be a warrior, she was also sad she would lose her only son and companion, to the city and courtly life.

She cried as the warrior woodcutter and Kintarō the warrior to be set out for the capital. But she swallowed her tears and bade her son farewell, knowing he would someday return as a samurai, and care for her when she was an old woman.

But Kintarō, who saw only the glory and glamour of samurai life, was rapt with joy. "I will be a samurai! A samurai!" he said to himself after he had put several titles before his name to see how they would sound.

"Master Kintarō? Hmm. Kind of plain," he thought. "Sir Kintarō? That has a nice ring to it. Lord Kintarō? Ooooh..."

A squirrel, another of Kintarō's animal friends, had heard the whole episode from just beyond the door. He ran to tell the others what he had heard, and within moments all of Kintarō's animal friends gathered on the path to the capital to say goodbye to their companion.

They bowed low before the general and waved as they joked with their friend. "Don't go forgetting your animal friends just because you're becoming a samurai, Kintarō," they called as the two disappeared into the woods down the trail to Kyoto.

The general sang all the way to the capital, and told Kintarō of some of his most glorious adventures. He warned the lad of the dangers that lie on the road leading to the two swords of the samurai, and he spoke of the manners of court so the boy would have some idea of how to handle himself before persons of importance. Sadamitsu was very happy, for in Kintarō he thought he had found the strongest warrior in all Japan—or at least the boy with the potential of being the strongest warrior in all Japan.

When they arrived in Kyoto, Sadamitsu left the boy and called on his lord. He told Lord Raikō the story of his first encounter with the boy and of the arm-wrestling match that ended in a draw, then he gave his lord and leader his analysis of the boy and his potential. The great leader was pleased and intrigued by the tales, and called immediately to meet the boy.

The meeting went well, and Kintarō was welcomed into the world of warriors-in-training.

Over the years, Kintarō surpassed his teachers' expectations, meeting every challenge and passing every test put before him. More importantly, he learned the ways of the court and shed his coarse countryside manners.

After mastering the skills of his chosen craft, Kintarō earned the right to wear the two swords of the samurai. Eventually, he rose through the ranks to command an elite group of warriors, hand-picked by Sadamitsu and his leader to fight evil and keep order in their kingdom.

Kintarō's exploits as a samurai are so well

known they don't bear recounting here, but let it be said that no matter how famous a warrior he became and no matter what lofty title he earned, Kintarō the samurai never forgot his allegiance to his lord, his debt to his teachers, and his love for his mother. The mightiest warrior in Japan remembered his days as a wild boy, and was always grateful to those who had helped him.

After one of his many legendary exploits against the demons of the land, Lord Raikō gave his warrior a beautiful palace made of the finest materials. Kintarō knew immediately it was time to bring his mother back to the capital, and he did so in a grand way, before the eyes of the very same enemies who had conspired to bring about to his father's untimely demise. These same enemies had long ago seen the folly of

clashing with Kintarō and had done their best
to make amends for their past wrongs.

Kintarō's mother lived with her son in the
capital to the end of her long happy life. When
she died, she died happily, knowing her dream
had come true.

Sannen Netarō—
Japan's Rip Van Winkle

Long, long ago, there was a very poor farming village near a river called the Asagawa. One of the many farmers in the village was known as "Netarō", the "ne" part of which is written with the Chinese character for "sleep".

The name was apt, for Netarō was asleep everyday from dawn to dusk. While his neighbors were out sweating in the fields under the hot sun, Netarō was sure to be found snoring away in his cool, comfortable bedroom.

If any brave soul dared to try and wake Netarō up by shaking him or yelling at him, the sleepy farmer's only reply would be something like "I'm sleepy. I'm really, really sleepy. My body is too heavy to move, and I can't open my eyes at all. Let me sleep." Then he would drift right back to a deep, dreamless sleep.

His beard was thick and tangled, and his body always had a noticeable coating of dirt and dust on it. Worse, he and the worn-out old *futon* he kept wrapped around him were thick with fleas and lice. His home was a playground for rats and mice, but Netarō, always asleep, never noticed.

The children of the village loved Netarō, especially the little boys. Being little boys, oversleeping and getting dirty came to them naturally. But they were always scolded by their

mothers whenever they slept too late or came
home dirty. Netarō was something of an ideal
to them, a role-model in reverse. He could sleep
and get dirty at the same time, and **his** mother
wasn't there to complain to him.

One day they gathered as usual outside his
dirty house and sang songs about him, trying to
wake him up to play. The singing, as usual,
brought no response from Netarō, so they called
to him.

"Netarō-san, can you open your eyes yet?"
Silence. Netarō did not stir.

"Netarō-san, come play with us!"
But it was useless. No matter how they tried,
Netarō never heard their calls. All they heard
in reply was the *guu-guu-guu* of Netarō's snores
echoing through the house.

The children climbed on to his porch one after the other. Full of curiosity, they took a pole
and poked a hole in the sliding paper door that
opened onto the porch. They jostled and pushed
each other to each take their turn staring into
what they thought of as the house of wonder.

"Will you look at that! He's slipped out of his
futon and rolled halfway across the room, but
he's still sound asleep."

"Get out of the way. It's someone else's
turn."

"Wow, you're right! He must really toss and
turn to get that far from his *futon*."

The children giggled, trying to keep their
laughter quiet. But they could not contain

themselves, and soon they were rolling around on Netarō's dirty porch, laughing so hard and loud tears came to their eyes.

The laughter managed to penetrate Netarō's veil of sleep. He groaned loudly "Uuuuuunnnnn", startling the children back into silence. He grasped at the *futon* covers he had kicked off, then rolled over on the floor.

"He's waking up! He'll be mad when he sees the hole in the door. Let's get out of here! Run!"

Netarō woke up, flustered, and jumped out onto his porch and ran out into the street. But the children had disappeared. From somewhere, Netarō heard their song again.

"Netarō, Netarō, wake up Netarō"

But the street was empty. Netarō went back to his house.

A huge black crow dropped out of the sky and landed in the garden, which had grown into a jungle long ago. It settled on a rack that once had been used to dry clothes in the sun. The black bird wobbled on the rack, then turned its head to Netarō's house.

"Caw, caw," it bellowed. Its voice was quite loud. "Fool, caw, fool."

A turtledove replied from a hill nearby with "ti-ti-paa, ti-ti-paa, fool, ti-ti-paa."

But the only reply from the house was the *guu-guu* of Netarō's snores.

Every day was the same. No matter how the children teased him, no matter how even the birds of the sky laughed at him, Netarō went back to sleep as if nothing had happened. Spring came and went, summer passed into autumn and changed into winter, and all the while Netarō continued his slumber.

From time to time he would open his eyes. He drank a little water and ate a little food, but all the time he was awake, just as all the time he was asleep, Netarō was thinking. He thought with all his powers of concentration. He thought with all his might about a most important thing.

Netarō had been a very good farmer before he became the Netarō he was now. He rose every morning before the crack of dawn and tended his fields until it was too dark to see. In those days, his fellow villagers held him in the highest esteem.

"He works so hard," they said. "He's sure to be a great man someday."

But Netarō had always been very poor, which was a problem, especially in his village. In Netarō's village there was no nearby source of fresh water. Without water, and lots of it, it is impossible to grow the most appealing crop, rice. The problem was compounded by frequent droughts that hit the area. Every year the villagers prayed to the gods for rain so the year's crops would have some chance of growing.

But rain rarely fell when the village's farmers needed it. The rice they worked so hard to plant would start to grow, young sprouts of green would begin to poke through the dry, cracked earth, but without water, the buds quickly turned a sickly brown and died.

To make a bad situation worse, the area was

under the control of a greedy, ill-tempered county governor. Every fall, when the meager crop was collected from the fields, the governor would visit each house and collect over half of each farmer's yield for property taxes.

Many county governors remembered their humanity when they performed their duties, and they would be fair and lenient when they collected the tax. If the year's harvest was poor, they would defer the tax until the next year, or the next year, or until the farmer could pay the tax. But the governor for Netarō's county was an evil man who always tried to collect the full amount of taxes, even when he knew it would leave the farmer and his family with nothing to eat.

Netarō and his fellow farmers knew that no matter how hard they worked, it would never amount to anything, and this thought troubled Netarō so much he could not sleep no matter how long and hard he sweated in the fields.

One year, Netarō decided it was time for a change. He spent all his savings to buy seeds of the best rice he could find. He worked hard to raise the seedlings and he filled his land with sprouts. For a time it looked as if his crop would break all records in his region.

But a mild spring was followed by a dry summer, which turned into a drought. Every single one of Netarō's young seedlings turned yellow and died. Netarō cried and cried for days. He ignored anyone that tried to console him, murmuring complaints about the stupidity of farmers and the greed of the tax men.

"Stupid, stupid farmers. Dumber than the earth they dig up. Year after year growing crops they know are going to die because there'll be no water. Even when the crop is fair they know the tax man will take as much as he can. They give it all to him without a word of complaint, knowing he'll only get fat off his take while they work their lives away. Yet they sweat and toil from dawn to dusk. What fools...

"If they complain, they get beaten up or tossed in prison. If they cut the amount they plant, they're cutting their own throats. What can be done to rid ourselves of the tax man once and for all?"

After some thought, Netarō decided his strategy would be to sleep. He put his plan into action at once, sleeping through the day. He slept all day long, and the next day, and the next.

In Netarō's mind there was no other way. Farmers did not have the status the county governor did, and they knew they would surely lose in any direct confrontation with authority. So the only way to win was through wile and deception.

To just quit farming was a dead-end road, because quitting meant no food, which meant there would be no way to keep oneself alive, not to mention that there would be no way to pay property taxes. "But a lazy man," thought

Netarō, "wouldn't need much food, right? No
need for energy when the most strenuous thing
you're doing is rolling over in bed, right?" A
strategy grew in Netarō's mind.

He continued to sleep as if he were ill, day in
and day out. "When the governor comes around
demanding his taxes, there'll be nothing for him
to take! Yes, that's the way—sleep and sleep
and sleep."

When his neighbors noticed Netarō was no
longer working his fields they began to wonder
about him. "He must have worked too hard.
He's just tired," they thought.

But as the days passed into months they
thought he had lost his mind. "The poor man,
he must have worked so hard his brain burned
in the hot sun." As a joke, someone started calling him Netarō, and the name stuck.

When the governor learned Netarō would
pay his taxes no longer, he immediately paid a
call on the young man. He let himself in when
Netarō failed to answer his calls at the doorway.
Finding Netarō asleep in his *futon* in the middle
of the day, the governor and his tax collectors
tried talking to him, then yelling at him to wake
him up. All their efforts came to naught, and
the governor grew angrier by the second. He
grabbed the sleeping man by the shoulders and
tried to shake him awake, but Netarō's only response was to groan and go right on sleeping.

The governor lost his temper and left in a
rage, vowing Netarō would die in his filthy little

house before he would ever set foot in it again. He and his tax collectors left with a large colony of Netarō's fleas and lice, and before they noticed their condition, they had infested their own homes as well.

Netarō had continued his drowsy hibernation for two years when the children of the village started singing about him. No one knew who had written the song, but all the children seemed to know it. It was a simple tune, teasing the former farmer for his lazy ways, but deep in their hearts, all the children envied the sleeper.

But, as we said earlier, Netarō was thinking all the while he slept. He thought of the most important thing, and he thought of it as hard as he could.

"No matter how evil the governor is, farmers have to work. No work equals no food. No food equals no farmer. But there is no water here. No water equals no food, which equals no farmers.

"There is the Asagawa, but the village and the only decent fields are high above the river. The river won't flow against gravity. What to do, what to do?"

Netarō slept for three years. On the morning of the third day of the third month of the third year of his hibernation, Netarō opened his eyes and jumped from his bed in a dynamic

burst of energy. Lice were scattered every-
where, and fleas abandoned his body, frightened because the warm, unmoving source of
their food for the past three years had become a
moving, active being.

Netarō did not notice them, nor did he pay
any attention to his tangly beard or filth-caked
body as he slipped on his sandals and went out
into the world.

"Netarō is awake!" cried villagers from their
fields when they saw him from the fields.
"Where could he be going?" they wondered.
"What is he doing?"

The villagers left their tools in the fields and
followed the bearded, dirty man. He walked at
a quick pace, heading toward the Asagawa. Fol-
lowing the river upstream, he walked through
one, then another of the villages next to his
own.

Finally, he stopped at a point where the
river ran much deeper and wider than it did
near his village. He turned to his exhausted fol-
lowers and said, "We need to get this water from
here to our village. How are we going to do it?"

The villagers, who had not heard more than
Netarō's snores for the past three years, were
startled and could not reply.

"*We* will get the water to our village, where
we will use it to grow rice." Netarō answered
his own question.

"Who is going to get us that rice?" a villager
asked.

"We are going to get that rice," said Netarō. "We are going to get that rice, and we are going to eat that rice until our bellies are full!"

The villagers looked confused. After a pause, one asked "How are we going to get the water to our village?"

"We are going to have water in our fields and we are going to have rice!" Netarō yelled at his fellow villagers. "We are going to grow rice, and we are going to grow rice successfully!"

"We are going to have more than enough rice for ourselves," he continued, "and for the tax man! We have got to stop growing grains and start going rice!"

The next morning, Netarō shaved and washed himself. As he washed, he heard the children start to sing in front of his house. Netarō went out to talk with them. Unable to run, they stared at the clean, wide-awake Netarō. "Why aren't you asleep?" asked one.

"I got tired of it," answered Netarō.

"What will you do now?" asked another.

"Work. I will work like you've never seen a man work before. I will work to get rice in my tummy and I will work to fill our bellies with rice."

The children murmured among themselves for a moment, then the leader of the little gang approached their idol. "We want to help," he said. "What can we do?"

"Follow me!"

Netarō and the children assembled the still confused villagers and started the task of getting water from the river to their fields. He gave his orders quickly, for he had had three years to make his plans. The villagers carried out the plan with great efficiency, with hope of a better life ahead.

The next spring, when it was time to plant rice seedlings, they had a more than ample supply of water from a channel leading directly from the high part of the river to their fields. The farmers rubbed their hands with excitement as they thought of the crops to come from these new fields.

And in the fall, Netarō's plan showed its true merit, as the farmers' fields were so fruitful they had to build new storehouses to hold all the rice! No one went hungry, and everyone had more than enough money for the governor and his tax men. Though he kept his nickname "Netarō", no one ever put his name and "lazy" in the same sentence again.

The villagers named their life-bringing channel after their slumbering hero. The channel is still there, and though it is no longer the lifeline it once was, it is still known as the "Netarō Waterway".

Urashima Tarō and the World Below

G₀ IN and listen to your grandfather," the mother told the boys. "He's about to tell you a story about Urashima Tarō and the sea kingdom."

The children took their places with their cousins and everyone gathered at grandfather's feet to hear his story for the umpteenth time. Every year at gatherings like this they surrounded the old man and begged him to tell his story. And every year grandfather told a slightly different tale, and every year the children listened without moving a muscle, rapt with wonder at the world grandfather created in the winter air.

"You've probably heard of Urashima Tarō, this town's greatest sailor, haven't you? Urashima Tarō?" Grandfather always began stories this way, speaking as if he was letting his audience in on a secret he and he alone knew.

"Urashima Tarō hailed from this very town, my boys, this very town. The most famous figure of these parts and he was from this little town." You could hear the pride in his voice. You knew he was just warming up, checking to see what kind of audience he had.

"Yes, yes. He lived near those hills by the bay, near where the road forks off to the city one way and the mountains the other."

"Yes, yes," he drifted into his tale. "He was an excellent fisherman in what was a town of excellent fishermen. He could take in what was a whole day's catch for other fishermen in half a day. Why, he was so good he could just drop anchor out there and the fish would jump into his boat. They knew, you see, that they didn't stand a chance against Urashima Tarō, so they'd throw themselves on his boat and beg for mercy. Soon there'd be so many fish on that boat he'd have to throw some of 'em back."

Here, Grandfather paused and took a sip of his tea. "Yeah, the fish he threw back could've fed the town several times over."

"That Urashima was so good his father could retire at an early age and turn over the business to him. He lived with his parents, you know. Took good care of them like your folks do me."

"But," he went on, "Urashima was even more famous in these parts for his kindness. Yes, for his kindness."

Grandfather looked at his audience for doubters and, finding none, continued.

"He wouldn't hurt any living thing, nosiree. A gentle man was he. Wouldn't even kill mosquitoes in the summer, and you know how they can get around here."

"Loved animals. Loved 'em. All kinds. Being both a fisherman and an animal lover, Urashima was especially popular with the cats in the area. He always had some little snack for them when they dropped by making the rounds."

Grandfather took a sip of tea and continued:

One day when he was out in the town, Urashima Tarō came upon some boys beating a turtle.

One boy was kicking at it while another was throwing pebbles at it. A third boy swatted its legs with a stick whenever the turtle tried to stick them out of the shell.

Urashima hated this. Of all the sins he could think of, abusing animals had to be the worst. He remembered his childhood, when

other boys had teased him for not joining them when they kicked dogs, threw rocks at cats and played their other mean little boy games.

These boys were at about the age where it's the thing to go around abusing animals. Urashima knew they weren't evil little children, but he couldn't stand to see the helpless turtle getting battered and pounded like it was.

"You there," he cried out. "What do you think you're doing? Leave that turtle alone and get out of here."

"It's our turtle," said the boy throwing stones. "We found him. We can do what we want to with him."

"And we want to kill him," said the boy with the stick.

"Why? What could a turtle have done to you?" asked the fisherman.

"That doesn't matter now, does it?" said the boy with the stones again. "It's our turtle and we'll do as we please."

They started to torture the turtle again, proud they had taken a stand against a grown-up and won.

But Urashima Tarō was not a man to give up easily. He knew he couldn't stand by and watch the boys beat the turtle to death. So he tried a different approach.

"It's your turtle, is it?" he asked the boys. "I think I'd like to buy your turtle from you. How about that?"

The boys stopped their abuse and looked at the fisherman.

He took the opening and quickly pressed his advantage. "Here, you take this and run along," he said, pressing a small coin in each boys hand. "Think of all the good things you can buy with this."

Visions of toys and sweets filled their little heads and the boys forgot all about the turtle and their "game". Without even thanking Urashima, the boys ran off for the market and left the man with the turtle.

"I'm sorry those boys beat you, turtle," said Urashima Tarō to his new companion. "They don't mean much. They're just at that age. You'll be all right now. I'll take you back to the sea."

The fisherman picked the turtle up and gently carried him to the shore. There he walked down the beach until he came to a nice secluded place to set the turtle free.

"Here you go, my friend. Please don't come back. I could save you this time, but I may not be around to help you again."

The turtle poked its head from its shell. When it realized where it was, it struggled to its feet and slowly crawled toward the water.

"Good-bye, turtle," said Urashima. He stayed and watched until the turtle had crawled through the surf and disappeared.

The next day, Urashima set sail and went

fishing as he always did. He said hello and good morning to the other fishermen as they eased out of the little town's harbor into the fishing grounds.

Somehow Urashima the fisherman felt happier, stronger, even lighter than usual. He turned the rudder with ease as he guided it through the seas. He felt as if all the worries of his life had left him. He felt so spirited, so healthy that he could live a thousand years.

He sailed out beyond most of the other fishermen, as was his custom. He was a great fisherman, but he was also an excellent sailor. Few of the other fishermen in the town would go as far out as he.

"There are monsters!" they would say. They tried to persuade him not to go to far out to sea to hide their own poor seamanship and cowardice.

"Urashima, don't you think you should be more careful? The sea-devils will get you if you go too far away from the shore. Then who would take care of your family?"

Urashima, being too kind to laugh at them, just ignored their foolish talk.

The weather was beautiful as Urashima circled around, trying to find a good spot to drop his nets.

As he circled, he thought heard a faint voice calling to his name. "Urashima! Urashima Tarō!" The voice was soft, as though one of the

town's fishermen had followed him to the
deeper seas. But Urashima turned and saw
only the empty sea.

He turned back to his nets, mending this
and straightening that before casting them into
the sea. But no sooner had he turned his back
than the voice began anew.

"Hey! Urashima! Down here?" the voice
called.

Alarmed, the fisherman dropped his nets
and slowly, carefully stuck his head over the
side of his ship.

There he saw a green sea-turtle, much like
the one he had saved only the day before.

"Greetings, Urashima! You have chosen a
fine spot for your day's fishing. This is one of
the richest fishing beds in these parts. You're
sure to have a nice catch today," said the turtle.

Urashima Tarō was a kind and gentle man,
and he understood the ways of animals. He
wasn't surprised that animals could talk, but
that they spoke Japanese just like you or me
surprised him. And if they could speak, why did
they wait until now? Why had they never done
so sooner?

"Hello, Mr. Turtle," Urashima hailed. "Are
you the same turtle I helped yesterday?"

"Yes, indeed," the turtle nodded. "I came to
thank you for saving my pitiful little life."

Urashima wasn't sure of proper etiquette
for receiving a turtle, but nevertheless asked,
"Would you like to come aboard?"

"Ah, thank you, don't mind if I do," replied the sea-turtle.

"Would you like something to smoke," asked

the fisherman. But he realized in mid-sentence, "Oh, you don't smoke do you?"

"I quit, actually," said the turtle. "But if you have a little *sake*, I wouldn't mind a little sip or two."

"I'm afraid I don't drink. Would you like some dried fish? I caught these a few days ago and they've been drying out on the deck here."

"Excellent," smiled the turtle. "Don't mind if I do."

After some small talk about cruel little boys and the fine weather, the sea-turtle looked straight at Urashima and asked, "Have you ever seen Rin Gin?"

"Rin Gin? I've heard of it. My mother used
to tell me tales of the King of the Sea. Rin Gin
was his palace was it not?"

"Is, Urashima, is," corrected the turtle.
"Present tense."

"But that was a fairy tale. Mothers always
tell their kids stories like that to..." Urashima
stopped himself.

'Here I am,' he thought, 'talking to a sea-
turtle. Surely stranger things can happen in
this world.'

The turtle interrupted his thoughts. "But
you haven't seen it, have you."

"Well, no."

"Would you like to? I owe you my life, and I
like to think it's worth at least that much."

"Well, I..."

"It *is* one of the most spectacular sights in
all creation, my dear Urashima," the turtle cut
him off. "You really shouldn't miss it. I would
be pleased, enthralled even, to act as your
guide."

"But I am a fair swimmer at best, and Rin
Gin would have to lie at the bottom of the sea,
would it not?"

"It would, it would," answered the turtle.
"But you have me, your guide. Trust me. Follow me. You can ride me. We'll be there before
you know it. Don't worry about the water or
drowning or anything—it's all been arranged."

"But you're so small," Urashima protested.
"How can I ride you?"

Without a word, the turtle slipped off the deck into the water. When Urashima leaned over the side of the ship to look, he saw the turtle had grown somehow. Now his shell was at least eight feet around.

"Well?" the turtle looked up. "Are you coming?"

Down, down, down the turtle dived into the depths of the ocean. Yet as deep as they dove, Urashima's clothes remained as dry as if they were on land. And true to his guide's word, the water had no effect on Urashima's breathing.

They continued on for so long that Urashima lost track of time—did they dive for hours? Days?

Eventually the darkness of the ocean floor parted and Urashima saw a great gate. It's size and beauty captivated Urashima, who forgot for the moment that this was only the outer gate of Rin Gin, the Palace of the King of the Sea. The palace itself was off in the distance, a much more spectacular structure.

The turtle stopped and asked Urashima to dismount. "From here, we walk."

The man and the giant turtle walked up to the gate, where a fish acted as the gate's sentry. The fish recognized the turtle, and stood aside.

"This is Urashima," the turtle said to the sentry, "of Japan. He is to be welcomed warmly and treated with the utmost respect."

The sentry stood aside and the pair walked

through the gate. Another fish went before them to spread the word of their arrival. Other fish came and joined them as they walked down the path to the inner keep of the Sea King.

"Welcome, Urashima," hailed a giant squid, and a school of tuna echoed the cheer. A great crab bowed low and an octopus waved all eight arms in greeting.

Urashima, however, was very uncomfortable with all the attention he was receiving. What did he, a fisherman, know about court manners and the like? But his mind took this all in without panic, without fear. It was as if he were having a dream where he knew he was dreaming; he felt safe knowing that it didn't matter what he did, because he thought he could wake himself up whenever he chose.

They were led to the great doors of the inner keep of the palace, where they were asked to wait for a moment. Then the doors were opened and a elderly, well-dressed crab welcomed them into a spacious hall.

"Your highness, I present Urashima Tarō of Japan," he cried, and the doors were shut behind them.

The turtle had quietly moved aside, leaving the fisherman alone in front of a grand throne. On the throne was a princess so beautiful Urashima was unable to speak. The deep greens and reds of her royal robes shimmered in the light of the great hall, and the deep black of her long hair first caught, then held Urashima's attention so that the turtle was forced to cough to remind the fisherman to bow in the presence of the Sea Princess.

Urashima bowed deeply, but was held fast by the princess' charms, too captivated to be embarrassed.

"Urashima Tarō," the princess spoke. Her voice was as beautiful as she. "I welcome you to my father's palace with a gratitude beyond bounds."

"Yesterday you first saved the life of a turtle, then you set it free. I am most grateful for your generous act because I was that turtle."

Urashima looked over at the turtle, who smiled back at him, admitting he had tricked Urashima into coming to Rin Gin.

"Mr. Turtle has played his role very well," she

continued, "and I am grateful to him for his part in bringing you here. Thank you, Mr. Turtle."

The turtle took this as permission to leave and excused himself, bowing. Urashima was alone with the princess and her retainers.

"I would like to show my gratitude to you, Urashima," the princess continued anew. "My father's kingdom is enchanted, and all who live here enjoy eternal youth. I would like to invite you to live here forever, to stay young forever."

"If you like," she added, "I will be your bride."

Here, the cool with which Urashima had handled previous events—traveling to the sea floor with a talking turtle and so on—evaporated. It was replaced with bewilderment and surprise.

"You'd, you... marry... forever?" He tripped over his words at the thought of marrying such a beautiful woman, not to mention living with her forever in eternal youth.

"I am inviting you to stay here forever as my husband, to stay young for eternity." The princess spoke slowly to make sure Urashima understood her words.

Urashima stopped a moment to regain his composure. "Yes," he said, "I am very thankful, very grateful! I would love to stay here with you forever. The palace is peaceful and beautiful, and you, you are surely the most beautiful woman I have ever seen, awake or in my dreams. I, I.... Yes, I would like to stay!"

The princess waved to a swordfish retainer, who disappeared behind a curtained wall. Then, the main door to the great hall opened and the retainer returned leading a royal procession of fish in ceremonial robes of the court. The fish carried trays of sushi and sashimi and other delicacies of the sea and set them before Urashima and the princess, making preparations for a great wedding feast.

Here one of the older children in Grandfather's audience broke the storyteller's spell.

"But, Grandfather," the child interrupted, "the fish ate other fish?"

"The fish carried trays? How did they carry the trays? Do some fish have hands?" queried another.

"Shhhh!" warned someone's mother and someone's aunt. "It's rude to interrupt! Don't stop Grandfather in the middle of his story!"

"No, no," said Grandfather. "It *is* an important question." But one that would not be answered, as Grandfather dove right back into his tale as soon as he had acknowledged the interruption.

Now, where were we? Ah, yes, the feast. A tremendous feast was held. The whole sea kingdom was called together for the celebration, for the princess was the Sea King's only child and the king himself was happy to add Urashima to his family.

There was wine and drinking and toasting. A school of sea fish sang songs and gold fish and silver-colored fish danced to entertain the party. The palace was normally a very beautiful place, but for this occasion it was decorated in the richest fashion, with greens and golds and other colors to give the whole palace a gay and festive atmosphere. It was, in short, a celebration the likes of which had never before been seen in the underwater world.

After the feasting and celebrating within the palace, the princess suggested Urashima tour the rest of her father's palace, and Urashima readily agreed.

Though the whole palace itself was beautiful beyond words, one part that struck Urashima as particularly striking was the outer garden. It surrounded the palace completely, and was divided into four regions, one for each season of the year.

To the north, Urashima could gaze upon a winter's garden scene. He saw snow-capped hills and trees lightly dusted with a glaze of snow. In the distance, a pond was covered with a sheet of ice, and Urashima shivered just looking at the scene.

The south garden, directly opposite the winter garden, was full of the lush greens of summer. Cicadas droned on during the day as a clear summer sun warmed the land. At night, crickets chirped as fireflies lit across a stream.

The garden to the east of the palace was full

of plum and cherry trees, all with their blossoms ablaze in color. The air was alive with
birds, flittering from one part of the garden to
the next in a happy chase.

And the garden west of the Sea King's palace was no less colorful, as the greens of the
eastern garden had passed on to the reds,
browns and yellows of autumn.

Every moment he spent in the great kingdom Urashima discovered something new and
beautiful, something wonderful or something
amazing. He was so absorbed in the splendor of
the palace that he soon forgot all about his old
life above the waves back in Japan. But after
three days he remembered the old Urashima
Tarō and his parents waiting for him.

"Ah, my parents must be worrying about

me," he thought to himself. "I set sail three days ago and have not returned. Surely they think I have died at sea."

Urashima liked the little village, but given a choice, he would have traded his old village life for his new life in the sea palace without a second thought. But deep in his heart he was aware of his love for his parents, if not his duties as their only son.

"Who will take care of my parents if I am not there?" he thought. And with that thought, he set about making hasty preparations for his return to the world above the sea.

He went to the princess and spoke to her. "I don't want to seem ungrateful, but I must ask to return to my village."

"What? But... are you somehow unhappy in this palace? Are you unhappy in your life with me? Is something wrong with your life here?" Having married Urashima only three days before, the princess was surprised and hurt.

Urashima explained his worries for his family and his responsibilities as their only son. The princess was disappointed, but she respected Urashima's loyalty to his parents and gave him permission to return.

"You would not stay even one more day with me?" asked the princess.

"Do not worry, my princess," said Urashima. "I only want to see how they are. I will return here, to you and this world after one day. Please wait for me."

The princess asked Urashima to wait while she brought out a parting gift for him.

"Please give my regards to your mother and father. And as a token of our love, please take this with you." She gave him a small lacquered box of the deepest green, inlaid with mother of pearl. It was tied shut with a cord of silk and red tassels.

"You have given me so much. Love, riches, eternal youth.... I cannot take this."

"Please, return with it, to remember me."

"I could hardly forget you, my princess, but what is this box?"

"This is the *Tamatebako*, the Box of the Jeweled Hand. It is a very special box, and what is inside it is even more precious. But you must never open it, no matter what happens. Never! Please promise me you will never open it."

Urashima promised, and the princess and her retainers followed the fisherman through the spectacular gardens to the edge of the palace, where Urashima again met Mr. Turtle.

He quickly hopped on the turtle and began the journey back to the surface. He turned and waved farewell to his princess until she first became a tiny dot on the horizon, then vanished in the distance.

The trip back to Japan seemed endless, as Urashima's heart was torn by the separation from his bride. But finally, the turtle surfaced and dropped Urashima off near the bay where

the fisherman first released the turtle/princess.

Here Urashima was gripped by a strange sensation. As he gazed upon his native land he felt something was not quite right, something was different.

He walked from the cove into the heart of the town and was startled. The landscape was as he remembered, but the people that passed him looked different, He didn't recognize their faces, and their clothes were in a different fashion.

He found the path to his parents' home as he remembered it, and there was a house where his should have been, but it was not his house. It was not the same house.

Urashima called out, "Father? Father, I am home. I have returned from the sea. I am not dead."

The door opened and a strange man, not Urashima's father, came out.

"Could my family have moved suddenly?" Urashima thought to himself. "But the house itself is different. What has happened?"

"Excuse me," said Urashima to the man in front of the strange house. "Until a few days ago I lived on this very spot. I am Urashima Tarō. Could you tell me what has happened to the family that lived here?"

The man stared at Urashima with a mixture of surprise and irritation. "What was your name again?"

"I am Urashima Tarō, the fisherman."

"Surely you are joking," the man's face turned red. "Or you are mad. Leave me be, and waste no more of my time. Away! Go, get along."

"No!" Urashima cried. Then he lowered his voice. "No, I am not joking and I am certainly not mad. I am Urashima Tarō."

"Look, a man named Urashima Tarō lived in this village once. He was a fisherman, and a pretty famous one at that. But that was about three hundred years ago. You don't look that old."

"*You* are joking, not me. Please tell me what I want to know."

"You may be who you say you are, but the only Urashima Tarō I've ever heard of in this village lived three hundred years ago. Perhaps you are a ghost?"

"No, fool. I am not a ghost. I have feet, see?"

Urashima stamped one foot on the ground with a thud, then the other. (Japanese ghosts don't have feet, and have to drift from place to place.) "See?"

"I've told you all I know," said the man, growing visibly irritated. "If you want to check for yourself, go to the village office and check the city records. Now leave me alone. I'm a very busy man, you know."

With that, the man went back into his house and left Urashima in the street, puzzled, confused, and more than a little bit frightened.

Urashima wandered the streets and saw that though the shape of the village was as he remembered it, the buildings were different. The people were different, their clothes were different, even the ships out in the harbor differed from Urashima's recollections. More than his time in the undersea world, his return to his hometown seemed like a strange dream.

The three days the fisherman had spent in the undersea world had been three hundred years in his old world. His parents, his friends, all the people he had ever known had died long ago, and the town now remembered the name Urashima Tarō only as a great fisherman and kind man who disappeared mysteriously at sea long, long ago.

Urashima wandered back to the beach. There was no reason for him to remain in this strange world. He should return to his beautiful princess and the palace of eternal youth as soon as possible.

But how? How was he to find his way back to the palace and his princess? He could not find his way back without help. Urashima the fisherman was lost and even more confused.

Finally, he remembered the *Tamatebako*, which he still carried in his left hand.

"I promised never to open it, I know. But now I have no hope. I'm sure she left a charm there to return me to her world should my return to this world be troubled. Surely I have nothing to lose by opening it now."

He struggled briefly, but the sadness over the loss of his parents, indeed, of his old life was too much for him. Added to his separation from the sea princess, Urashima was despondent. In his misery, the fisherman allowed himself to break his promise to the princess and open the box.

Slowly and gently, he untied the cords of silk that held the box shut. Three waspy arms of purplish smoke drifted from the box and clouded over Urashima's face. Then it dissipated and dissolved on the sea breeze.

Before he knew what had happened, Urashima Tarō, a young, muscular fisherman of twenty-four became a withered old man, with long white hair and scraggly whiskers. He aged three hundred years in an instant, and fell down dead right on the spot.

"Here is the moral of the story for you, young ones," Grandfather gave the children assembled before him a frightening stare.

"Keep your promises! Obey your elders! Respect and take care of your parents or you will lose everything! Now go out and play. And be good! Or else!" Grandfather looked up at his children, the parents of the children before him, and winked.

Hanasaka Jiisan

T HERE once lived an old man and his wife in some distant part of Japan. They were childless and lonely, and worried what might befall them without children to take care of them as they grew older. The fear and loneliness particularly affected the old man, and one day he got it into his head that he was going to town to get himself a child. He hadn't worked out exactly how he was going to get a child—he was too kind to just kidnap one, too poor to adopt one, and he wouldn't stoop to buying a child—but he knew it was high time he did something, and something told him to go to town.

On the way to the town the old man came across a puppy in a grove of pine trees. It was completely white from the tip of its nose to the end of its tail, and it spoke to the old man. "*Wan, wan*! Where are you headed, old man?"

"*Ara*, what a cute little puppy you are. I'm off to town to get me a child."

"Is that so? What do you want a child for?"

"My wife and I are getting pretty old, my young pup. In a few years there will be no one to care for us. And the house seems so empty with only the two of us..."

"Well, what if you were to take me as your child?"

The question caught the old man off guard. He stood and thought for a moment. "How about this," he answered. "You wait right here while I go on to town and look for a child. If I don't find one, you can come home with me as my child."

The puppy agreed and the old man went on down the path to the town.

First, the old man wandered around the town's marketplace asking people for their children. The bluntness of his appeal surprised and frightened the villagers, who wondered why he wanted their children. Not surprisingly, more than a few of the townspeople called him rude names and threatened to have him run out of town if he persisted in asking for children.

The man continued his efforts at the local shrine and other town centers, but no one was willing to part with a child. He thought of asking door-to-door just to make sure he had asked everyone in the town, but it was growing late. Lonelier than before, the man left the town.

On the way back, he remembered the puppy's offer and stopped at the pine grove.

"How did it go, old man?" asked the puppy, though he could see the old man returned as alone as he had left.

"No good. No good at all. Nobody wanted to give me their children, not even one. So, you'll be my child?"

The dog danced around in a little circle, whimpering and woofing with joy. "I'd love to!" he said, wagging his tail furiously.

The old man and the puppy went home together. At first, the old man's wife was a bit put out at the idea of a dog for a child, but the old man explained the situation, that no one was willing to give them a child and that they should be happy they had found a puppy so intelligent and handsome. The puppy also turned on the charm for the old woman, and eventually she grew fond of the dog.

They loved the puppy just as they would have loved a real child. They fed him at the table, feeding him the tastiest portions of fish and pork. They took care of his wounds and saw him through his illnesses. In the winter, he had a warm blanket spread out before the fire, and in the summer he always had plenty of water.

Before you could say *"wan-wan,"* the puppy grew into a fine dog, obedient and full of respect for his "parents."

One autumn day much like any other, the old man put on his blue work clothes, picked up his hoe and went out to tend the fields. As usual, the dog went with him to help however he could. That day the farmer was tending some fields high on a hill far from his home. He went straight to work hoeing and digging, while the dog wandered around the border of the field. The dog was sniffing for something, and every now and then he would stop and scratch at the ground.

Suddenly, the dog stopped sniffing and barked at his master. "Here! Here it is! Dig here!"

The old man was busy with his work. He couldn't stop every five minutes to dig up bones for his dog. But the dog would not give up. "Here it is, I tell you! Dig here!"

The man ignored him again, so the dog went over, grabbed the man's arm in his teeth and pulled him toward the spot.

"Okay! Okay! Enough already. I'm coming." The old man followed the dog's lead.

"Here it is! Dig here!" the dog said, and he began to claw the earth. The man did as the dog asked and soon heard the *skritch—skritch—skritch* sound of his hoe hitting metal. After a little more work the pair unearthed something shiny.

"Coins! Gold coins!" cried the man. The man picked up one of the coins and watched it glitter in the sun. "It's gold, dog. Gold!"

He scooped up all the coins and checked the soil for more. In all, the old man found about twenty gold coins—enough to make him and his wife comfortable for some years to come.

The old man was almost in tears with happiness when he thanked the dog. "Thank you! Thank you for leading me to this treasure!" Then, his work in the fields through, he put the coins in his pouch and went home.

The old man ran through the door to his home. His wife, coming in from the garden, looked as though she might scold the man and dog for tracking dirt into her clean house, but the man spoke before she could begin. "Look!" he cried to his wife. "Look what the dog found for us!" He showed her the coins and told her how the dog almost dragged him to the spot where the treasure was buried.

"What a remarkable dog!" marveled the woman. "You get a special treat tonight!"

The couple set the money on a table while they thought about places to hide it. While they were thinking, the woman next door came by to borrow some embers from the old man's fire. (The neighbors were lazy good-for-nothings, too irresponsible to keep their own fire going.) The first thing she saw when she came into the room was the pile of gold coins on the table. Natu-

rally, she asked about the coins; she knew her home was as poor as the old man's—how could he come into such wealth so suddenly?

The neighbor listened rapt with wonder as the old woman told the whole story about the coins. She was particularly surprised when she heard the dog found the coins, and she hurried home to tell her husband. She went home in such a hurry that she forgot the embers she came to borrow.

The old man next door listened to his wife recount the story. Bluntly put, he was a bad man. He was greedy and scheming, and when he heard of his neighbor's good fortune he thought not of his neighbor's good fortune—he was more concerned with getting some gold for himself.

He was more than a little jealous when he

heard his neighbor's dog had led him to the treasure. He hated pets, especially the white dog his neighbor kept. But when he heard the dog led his neighbor to a fortune in gold, he stroked his beard and thought aloud, "So if I get that dog, I can find gold of my own!" His wife started to return to the neighbors, again to borrow some embers for the fire, but her husband stopped. "I'll go myself," he said, and he went to visit his neighbor.

The old man, the owner of the dog, was a kind-hearted man. He knew that the neighbor was far from a model citizen. He also knew his neighbor hated dogs. But no matter how rude or scheming his neighbor might be, the old man could not refuse his request. The neighbor could not wait for the next morning, he said, he had to have the dog right away. The old man relented, so instead of having a special treat for supper, the great white dog had only a few bare chicken bones tossed from the neighbor's table.

The neighbor took the dog out to the fields early the next morning, hours before the sun came up. He wore his best clothes, for he was determined to look his best when he found his fortune.

He tied a rope around the dog's neck to keep it from straying. (The old man never used a leash of any sort!) "Let's go, dog!" commanded the neighbor. "Find me some gold!"

The dog did not move.

"Come on, dog!" the neighbor yelled. He yanked on the leash, jerking the dog around the field. "Is it here? Huh? Is the gold here?" No response from the dog. "Is it there, huh? Where is it? Come on, dog!"

The man grew angrier and angrier as the dog just wandered around the field, sniffing and snorting as if it were any normal dog out for a walk with his master.

Finally, the man lost his temper and struck the dog with his hoe. "Is it here, dog?"

The dog yelped with pain. "Dig if you want, or don't dig if you don't want to. That's all I can say to you."

The man took up the hoe and dug until he too hit something metallic. He dropped to the ground and clawed at the soil with his hands until he pulled metal from the earth. But instead of gold, the neighbor's metal was lead. Worthless, dirty lead that had a most foul smell about it.

Angered, the man struck the dog once more, and the two wandered around the fields again until the man's patience again wore thin. "Here? Here, dog?"

As before, the dog's reply was ambiguous. "Dig if you want to—I can tell you no more."

The man dug again, and once more he hit metal. And once again, he discovered—foul-smelling lead.

By now, the man's clothes were soiled with sweat and dirt from the work. The stench of the

lead was all over him. "Damned dog, you'll
make no fool of me!" The man yelled at the dog
and hit him again with the hoe. Then he struck
the dog with the sharp blade end of the hoe.
The dog howled with pain and his white coat
turned crimson with blood. Again and again
the man struck until the hoe was bloodied and
the dog howled no more.

When night fell and their dog still had not
returned, the good old man and his wife paid a
call on their evil neighbor. "Where is our dog?
We are lonely without him. Please give him
back to us now."

The evil neighbor was completely unruffled
as he told the old couple, "Oh, your dog. He was
a very, very bad dog. All day long we walked the
fields and he wouldn't bark. Not even a whim-
per. Then, when he finally did bark, I dug just
where he said, but all I found was worthless
lead. So I killed him. He was a worthless mon-
grel anyway."

"Oh," said the old man, and the couple returned home. The old man and his wife were so
kind-hearted they could not grow angry at their
neighbor, even when they learned of his greedy
cruelty, even when they learned he had slain
the dog they had taken for their son.

They went to the fields and brought home
the dog's bloodied body home. He had been a
good companion as a dog and a source of friend-
ship and love as a son. And he had uncovered

enough gold for them to live comfortably for the
rest of their lives. The least we can do, they
thought, is give him a proper burial in our garden.

The days went by and the couple lived comfortably, but in a lonely sadness without their
child. With some of the dog's treasure they
bought a tombstone and dedicated it to his
memory. They poured a cup of water on the
tombstone twice a day, just as they had given
water to their dog.

Before long, the couple noticed a plant growing from just behind the tombstone. It grew and
grew with tremendous rate, and within weeks
of the dog's death a mature tree stood just behind the tombstone.

The old man marveled at the wonder, the
tree that had so suddenly sprung up in his back-
yard. "It's getting to be a good size," he re-
marked to his wife. "What should we use it for?"

"It's a fine tree. But I'm not sure what we
should make from it. If nothing else, I need a
new mortar for grinding rice."

The old man cut the tree down and made a
fine mortar for his wife. There was more than
enough wood for the mortar, so he carved a
pestle as well. He decided to try it out before
presenting it to his wife, so he took a little rice
and started to grind away. He ground the rice
with the mortar and pestle somewhat absent-

mindedly, watching the birds in the garden, looking at the clouds floating by. After some time he looked down at the mortar. To his sur-

prise, it was full of gold flakes! Grinding rice with that mortar and pestle somehow turned the rice into little splinters of gold!

He called to his wife, and together they watched as he ground more rice into gold flakes! "What a wonderful thing!" they exclaimed.

They put a little pile of flakes in a bowl and had just started their supper when there was a knock on the door. It was their neighbor woman again, coming to borrow embers from their fire again.

The woman from the house next door came with a box for the embers and, of course, saw the bowl of gold flakes on the table. As before, she asked how the old couple had come to have a bowl full of gold flakes, and as before, the kind old woman was all too friendly and told the neighbor the tale of the mortar and pestle.

Of course, word of the magic mortar and pestle got back to the evil neighbor, who at once paid a "friendly visit" on his neighbors. You would think that after killing his neighbor's dog out of greed and spite that the evil neighbor would have second thoughts about visiting the kind old couple. But he was as shameless and greedy as the old couple was kind. He asked to borrow their mortar and pestle, and the old couple relented.

When the man returned to his home he immediately filled the mortar with rice and set about grinding. But try as he might, instead of gold flakes, the greedy man's grinding produced only a foul-smelling sand. He kept trying, with different types of rice, grinding gently and grinding with all his might, but all he was left with in the end was a bowl full of sand.

His eyes red with fury, the evil man yelled "What a worthless bowl! Away!" He threw the mortar with all his might and broke it against a rock in his garden.

The next morning the kind old man dropped by to retrieve the mortar. He found his neighbor in the garden with what looked a piece of a broken mortar bowl at his feet. He was making a fire and burning dead branches from the garden.

"Ah, you're here for your mortar, aren't you?" he asked the old man. The old man looked at the fire and nodded. "Don't waste your time. It was a worthless piece of trash anyway. When I tried to grind a little rice the only thing that would come out of it was stinky sand. So I broke it, and burned most of it."

"Well, what a waste," said the kind old man. "I will take the ashes back with me. They remind me of my dog." Sadly, the old man put the ashes from the burnt mortar and pestle in his pouch and returned home.

The man went to his own garden, where he took a handful of the ashes and threw them up into the air. The wind took them and scattered them all around the garden, mostly around an old withered mulberry tree. When the ashes hit the tree, it instantly burst into life all green and full of flowers and blossoms.

"This is truly special," thought the old man. "Ashes that can make withered plants bloom again!"

Without a word to his wife, he took his pouch of magic ashes and went straight into town crying "Make withered trees blossom! I can make dead and dying trees bloom full of life again! Let me take care of your gardens! I am *Hanasaka Jiisan*, the man who can make withered trees bloom with beauty and life."

As circumstance would have it, the *daimyō* of the region happened to be passing by as the old man went crying through the streets. "Old man," the *daimyō* said to the old man, "the cherry trees in the castle garden have been withered and sickly for some years now. Let's see what you can do for them."

"Certainly, my lord. My services are not at all expensive," replied the old man, and he followed the *daimyō* back to the castle.

He was shown to the castle garden, where he announced for all to hear, "I am *Hanasaka Jiisan*, the old man who can make withered plants bloom again, who can bring dead plants back to life." At the center of the garden, he found several cherry trees, all withered and dying. He went straight to work, sprinkling a little of the ashes of the mortar on first the upper branches, then the middle and lower branches, then on the very trunks of the withered trees. When he had finished, he stood back and asked the *daimyō*, "Now, watch carefully, my liege."

Slowly at first, the brown and withered trees turned green. Then, with a bright explosion of color, the tree was alive with healthy pink cherry blossoms. New branches burst from what had been dried wood, and these branches also bore bright pink blossoms. The audience that had gathered to watch the old man work murmured in astonishment. The *daimyō* was impressed.

"This is most spectacular," he told the old man. "You have earned a fine reward." He sent

his retainers to the treasury, and they returned
with a great chest of gold coins. It was so laden
with gold the *daimyō* had to lend the happy old
man a pack-horse to carry the great chest home.

The greedy neighbor was seething with rage
when he saw the old man return with his chest
of gold. "I can do that," he thought, and he filled
a pouch with some of the ashes left from the fire.
"Anyone can do that."

The evil neighbor took his pouch and went
through the town crying, "I can make withered
trees bloom again! I can rejuvenate your tired,
old plants! I am the man who can save your
plants. I am *Hanasaka Jiisan!*"

One of the *daimyō*'s retainers heard the
man and called him over to speak to him. "You
are the man who can bring withered plants
back to life?" he asked.

"I am no other. Lead me to your ailing
plants, allow me to tend to your withering
trees."

"We forgot to mention one other tree we'd
like you to save. Please come back to the castle
with me"

"Certainly," said the evil man with and evil
twinkling in his eye. "My prices are reasonable."

The man followed the retainer back to the
castle, where he was shown to the garden. The
daimyō, he was told, could not be disturbed, but
he was very anxious about his tree. The re-

tainer led the man to what was the largest cherry tree in the garden. It was very dry and withered, and any other gardener would have cut it down and used it for furniture or firewood long ago. But the *daimyō* had special memories associated with this tree, and he had ordered that gardener to do whatever had to be done to save it. The tree, the retainer explained, was to be revived at all costs.

Word of the wonders of *Hanasaka Jiisan*'s earlier performance had spread quickly through the castle. On hearing the great man had returned for another show, the castle serving staff and all the castle gardeners assembled to watch the man work his magic.

Carefully, gingerly, the greedy man climbed to the top of the ladder leaning on the sickly brown tree. He spread his ashes on the upper limbs, then he worked his way down the tree spreading the ashes. Finally, he sprinkled an especially generous portion of ash around the base of the trunk.

Then, with all the castle staff watching the tree for a sign of life, a splash of new color— nothing happened. The man waited, the retainers waited, the staff waited, and nothing happened. The crowd waited for several minutes, but still, nothing happened. Then someone in the crowd remembered that when the kind old man had revived the trees on his earlier visit, the trees had burst into life in a matter of moments. The crowd realized that something was wrong, and the palace guards grabbed the evil old man.

"I am not *Hanasaka Jiisan!*" he cried. "I am only a poor old man! Please have mercy on me!"

But by now word of the impostor had reached the *daimyō*, who appeared from his balcony overlooking the garden. "Throw the impostor in prison!" he ordered the guards. Wailing all the way, the greedy man was carried off to prison.

On the other hand, the kind old man—the real *Hanasaka Jiisan*—lived comfortably with his wife for the rest of their lives. Thus are the rewards for kindness and virtue, and thus are the punishments for greed and evil.

Kaguyahime—Moon Princess Born from Bamboo

Long ago and far away, there lived a bamboo cutter (in Japanese, a *taketori*) and his wife. The bamboo cutter enjoyed his work, though he had never heard of a wealthy bamboo cutter. He relished the freedom he had to wander the forests in search of the precious wood, spending day after day in the wilderness. The thought of farming or working a trade appalled him, and he preferred to remaining poor to trading his freedom for a little money.

One autumn day while roaming the forests for bamboo, the man saw a brilliant light. It was most unusual, but the man felt no fear at all. Indeed, the light seemed to calm him, and he found himself strangely attracted to it. He followed his instincts and moved toward the light, which came from a thicket of bamboo hidden amidst the pines.

Normally, the discovery of a bamboo grove would have surprised the man, for as a bamboo cutter he thought he knew where all of the local bamboo thickets were, and he had never seen this one. But the light kept his mind on other things.

The light seemed to radiate from the center of the tiny thicket, from the largest bamboo tree in the grove. As if moved by forces beyond his control, the man walked to the glowing tree and

raised his axe. The tree fell with but one swing
of his blade, and there in the center of the hollow trunk sat a beautiful, tiny baby girl.

"A blessing from the gods," he murmured in
a voice not his own. He lifted the tiny child up
in the palm of his hand and gazed upon her face.
She was the most beautiful baby he had ever
seen! She did not stir or cry out when the
woodsman felled her tree, nor did she stir now
as he held her in his coarse hands.

Leaving the felled tree as it was, he returned to his poor home to show his wife his discovery. She was as dumbfounded as he, but she
interpreted the child's coming in the same way;
without realizing it, the words "a gift from the
gods" rolled from her lips as tears of joy rolled
down her cheeks.

She snatched the child away from her husband, who, because of his inexperience, was holding the child as he would a sack of rice. She held the child tenderly in her arms and wondered what they were to do with the child. The silent child smiled and the woman knew exactly what to do. Without a word between them, the bamboo cutter and his wife made up their minds to keep the gift from the gods as their daughter.

The next day, the bamboo cutter returned to the thicket where he found the baby. He went to retrieve the bamboo he had left there the previous day, half expecting to find another child. But as the forest seemed completely normal as he approached the thicket this time.

He left the path entered the bamboo grove and looked for the tree he had felled—but it was not there. More startling, the trunk of the tree was gone as well. There was no sign the trunk had been dug up, and the only footprints in the whole of the area around the grove were his own.

"Mysterious," he thought to himself. His thoughts were soon disturbed by another discovery. As he examined the ground for footprints, he discovered a small gold coin! Then his eyes found another coin. Crawling on his hands and knees to the second coin he discovered third one. Then another, and another, and another until he discovered a larger gold coin.

Dizzy with excitement, the man stood up and looked around the thicket. He found gold coins wherever he looked!

He gathered up all the coins and ran home again to his wife. As he ran, he thought only of his new daughter. "Now we can raise her properly!"

The next day, the bamboo cutter returned to the grove. Unsure of what to expect this time, he kept his eyes on the ground. Sure enough, when he entered the bamboo thicket he found just as before—full of gold coins of all sizes. Once more, the man filled his sack with coins and ran home. With just two days of these mysterious riches the bamboo cutter became the richest man in his part of the country.

The couple decided to call their child Kaguyahime, "hime" meaning princess. She grew as quickly as bamboo shoots up from the soil. After three months in the bamboo cutter's home, the beautiful baby girl had grown into an even more beautiful young woman. Word of her beauty spread quickly, and soon five princes came to the bamboo cutter's home from the capital to ask to marry his daughter.

The five were no ordinary princes. For weeks, the capital had been in an uproar over who was going to ask the princess, as Kaguyahime was known, for her hand in marriage. Fights broke out, duels were fought and blood ran in the streets before the forces of reason prevailed. Five young men from the capital would win the right to travel to the bamboo cutter's town to court the beautiful Kaguyahime, and those five would be selected through a series of contests and competitions.

The five princes that now appeared at the bamboo cutter's door were selected from over one hundred potential suitors, and had distinguished themselves in trials measuring their wit, strength, grace and knowledge.

Even after their selection the princes faced trials, for the road from the capital to Kaguyahime's home was long and difficult. They traveled for weeks, suffering illness and misfortune all along the way.

But the five princes had survived all their trials. Without stopping in the town, they went straight to the princess' home, where they visited Kaguyahime's father and asked for an audience with his now-legendary daughter.

The princes plied the bamboo cutter with gifts of gold, art and rare spices and food, and he in turn welcomed them warmly and with respect due their rank. But he refused to allow them to meet his daughter. "I cannot force my daughter to meet with you if she herself does not wish it," he told the princes.

The princes accepted this as only a minor setback, and together they left the bamboo cutter's home. But to show their devotion to Kaguyahime, all five of them vowed to wait outside her house until she agreed to see them.

The princes waited all that summer and fall, through heat and rain, mosquitoes and chill. They serenaded Kaguyahime with songs of their love and devotion. They wrote long, passionate love letters imploring the princess to do no more than allow them to gaze upon her beauty. But all their songs fell on deaf ears and all the letters were returned. Kaguyahime would have nothing to do with any of the five, and even with winter's snows approaching, she showed no signs of relenting.

Her father, however, was not as strong as she was. He asked his daughter if she would consider granting each prince an audience—if for no other reason than an audience followed by a flat rejection seemed to be the quickest way to send the princes back to the capital. The bamboo cutter did not want to see his daughter marry and leave his home—far from it, he was very much afraid of the loneliness he and his wife would feel without their daughter's company.

But Kaguyahime's father was a compassionate man. He remembered that during the rainy season and then during the typhoon season, the young princes had stubbornly maintained their vigil in front of the house. Each of them had at one point or another fallen victim to the elements and become seriously ill. With winter coming, it seemed only a matter of time before one or more of the devoted fools caught pneumonia or froze to death.

Thus it was on humanitarian grounds that Kaguyahime's father asked her to reconsider her rejection of the suitors.

"I do not wish to see any of the princes," she told her father. "But if you ask me to, father, I cannot refuse you."

The bamboo cutter thought of the well-intentioned princes with pity, and asked his daughter to grant them an audience.

Kaguyahime relented, but she stipulated that each prince had to earn the right to an interview. To earn the right, she decided, each prince would have to meet a challenge. The first prince's challenge was to bring the princess a Buddhist artifact, a stone bowl used by the Buddha.

The trail for the second prince was to travel to Mt. Hōrai far across the Eastern Sea, and return with a branch from a tree at the mountain's peak. This would be no ordinary branch, for the tree itself was made of gold. Its branches were of silver, from which grew fruit of diamonds, rubies and other precious gems.

The third prince was to travel to China for the skin of a fire-rat. The skin of a fire-rat was said to be magical, having such properties that it would not burn when placed in fire.

The fourth prince was assigned the task of winning a jewel that radiated five colors depending on the light that struck it. The job was complicated by the fact that the jewel was in the possession of a dragon famous for eating anyone who dared disturb its peace.

The challenge for the fifth prince was no easier: he was to find a swallow that had in its stomach a special shell.

Kaguyahime's father relayed the challenges to the princes and watched their expressions carefully. He could tell they were disappointed and disheartened with the enormous difficulties their challenges entailed, but none of the princes gave voice to his feelings. Not wishing to seem weak before his rivals, each prince made a great show of bravado and swaggered back to the town. But all the bravado was gone by the time each had returned to his own kingdom.

The first prince thought of the dangers he would encounter in traveling to the land of the

Buddha, the difficulties in finding the stone bowl in question and convincing its owners to part with it, and of the time the quest would take, and he thought of a different way to win the princess.

After waiting quietly in his kingdom for several years, he paid a visit to a Buddhist temple in a neighboring province. He convinced the head priest to sell him one of the temples great stone bowls and, thinking one stone bowl looks about the same as any other, he returned to the bamboo cutter's home to claim his interview.

He presented the bowl to the bamboo cutter, who was very surprised the prince had completed his quest in such a short time. He promised to give it to the princess that evening and asked the prince to return the next morning for his interview.

The princess was also surprised when she heard the first prince had completed his quest. She looked at the bowl very carefully, examining it for flaws and other marks only she could recognize. After no more than a few moments of examination, Kaguyahime saw through the prince's fraud. Shocked with her discovery, she dropped the bowl, shattering it into dozens of tiny pieces.

When the prince arrived early the next morning to claim his bride, Kaguyahime's father refused to meet with him. Instead, he sent a servant to give him the shattered pieces of stone. The first prince understood he had been discovered. He left without a word.

The second prince also realized the futility of the task Kaguyahime had chosen for him. And like the first prince, the second prince sought to win the princess through deception. Rather than risk his life on the treacherous Eastern Sea, he called on all his province's jewelers, goldsmiths and silversmiths to create a branch of the jeweled tree.

The task took several years. When it was finished, the prince called on the father and gave him the great branch. The bamboo cutter was amazed—never before had he seen such fine work! It was evidence of the prince's success, and he would have to allow him an interview with Kaguyahime.

The beauty of the branch, with glittering jewels budding from its bright silver base, impressed him so that he invited the prince to sit down. Resigned to the fact that this was the man that would take his daughter away, he talked with the prince to see what sort of man he was.

The two talked and enjoyed refreshments for some time, and the bamboo cutter seemed impressed with the prince's wit and intelligence. While they spoke, however, a messenger came to the bamboo cutter's home with a message for "the master". The bamboo cutter's retainers would not allow the messenger to disturb their master's discussions with the prince, but they agreed to give him the message.

A retainer entered the room where the two were discussing politics and the world. He begged his master's forgiveness, then handed him a note. The bamboo cutter read the note and saw immediately that it had been meant for the prince—his retainers had confused the messenger's master with their own. A gentleman does not read another person's correspondence and the bamboo cutter was a gentleman. But it was such a short note that he had read the letter before he could avert his eyes. It read:

Your Highness,
  We have delivered the jewel encrusted branch of silver and gold exactly as you ordered, yet you *still* have not paid us for our labor. We demand that you pay us immediately!

Respectfully yours,
*The XXX Province Smithies &
Jewelers Assoc.*

The bamboo cutter handed the letter to the prince and left the room. The interview was over and a second prince had been disqualified.

Like the others before him, the third prince sought to fulfill his quest through less than honest means. Rather than go to China and search for the fire-rat himself, the prince paid a sea captain to acquire one for him. Wisely, he paid the captain only a small part of the reward before he set sail, and promised to pay the remaining sum on the captains successful return.

After a few years, the captain returned with the skin of the fire-rat. He told the prince a long story of how he and his men went to great lengths to procure the skin, and how most of his men had died in combat with this villain or that monster. The prince listened intently, thinking how to use the captain's words as his own when the time came to tell the tale of the skin of the fire-rat to a rapt Kaguyahime and her father.

He paid the captain a handsome fee, in addition to ample condolence payments for the families of members of the captain's crew that had died on the voyage. Then he assembled his retainers and set out for the bamboo cutter's home.

Kaguyahime's father welcomed the third

prince guardedly. He had been fooled twice before and he did not want it to happen a third time. The prince began to tell him how he led his ship to China, fought these monsters and those villains and finally, after much hardship, won the precious skin of the fire-rat. But the bamboo cutter would hear none of it—he waved his hand to silence the prince before he could begin his tale.

Not at all discouraged, the prince dropped to one knee before the bamboo cutter and offered him the skin of the fire-rat. The bamboo cutter took the skin immediately, took it into the grand kitchen of his home and tossed into the cooking fire. The true skin of the fire-rat should have been impervious to all flame, but the prince's gift burst into a bright yellow flame as the first flame touched it. It burned brilliantly, and with a terrible smell.

The prince was truly surprised by this turn of events. "That scoundrel! I paid him a fortune in gold for that skin!" he cried. Realizing the shame of his outburst, the prince hung his head and left in disgrace.

The fourth prince was much too busy running his kingdom to spend the time and fortune required to find and kill the dragon with the multicolored jewel. Nor was the prince at all interested in risking his life in combat with such a fierce creature. Several of his retainers were so sure of themselves they convinced the prince they would have no trouble at all finding and killing the dragon for the prince. The prince had so much faith in himself that he paid his men in advance.

The men, however, were not as trustworthy as the prince had believed. They took the money and fled to an island far from the prince's kingdom. "Why should we risk our lives for something that probably doesn't even exist anyway?" they asked as they drank *sake* bought with the prince's reward money. "What do we care if the prince stays a bachelor for the rest of his princely little life?" they joked as they ate fine foods bought with the prince's reward.

After a few years, the prince realized he had been duped. He was livid with anger, and declared in a regal rage, "I can find that jewel if I have to. Who knows what calamities may befall my state in my absence. But if I have to find and kill the dragon *all by myself*, I will!"

And he tried valiantly: he ordered a ship to set sail at once for what he thought was the Isle of Dragons, ignoring what he thought were the foolish pleas of the ship's captain. In so doing, the prince set sail during that time of the year when the seas are at their roughest and the winds at their deadliest. The ship was caught in a storm and dashed upon the rocky shore of a lonely little island. The prince and the other few survivors were stranded for many years, during which the prince reconsidered his love for the beautiful Kaguyahime.

The fifth and last prince made the most earnest efforts of the lot. He spent years in his search for the swallow with a shell in its belly, and countless swallows lost their lives in his pursuit of the princess Kaguyahime. He was inventive, and quickly discovered that rather than killing swallows one at a time with his arrows, he could kill hundreds of birds with nets and other new devices he designed.

But after years of trying, he finally gave up and accepted his failure like all the other princes had done before him.

With the failure of each of the five princes, Kaguyahime and her parents lived a quiet, happy life for some time. However, the epic failures of the five princes drew the attention of all of Japan. Eventually, word of the five and their attempts to win the princess reached the Emperor's ears. Upon hearing of the immeasurable beauty of the princess Kaguyahime, the Emperor decided he wanted to see this great beauty with his own eyes.

Avoiding any nonsense with challenges and quests, the Emperor sent a messenger to the bamboo cutter asking him and his daughter to the Imperial Court. But even this was rejected by the beautiful princess.

Rather than getting angry, the Emperor found he was intrigued by her coquettish refusal to answer his request. He sent another messenger, this time with a summons ordering the princess to appear before him in the capital.

When the bamboo cutter read the summons, he wondered how Kaguyahime would reply. Her answer was more surprising than anything he had expected.

Kaguyahime asked her father to relay to the Emperor the message that she could not attend the Imperial Court and could not obey the Imperial Summons. If she left her home with the bamboo cutter and his wife, she would disappear like a wisp of smoke in the wind.

Once again, the princess' refusal only increased the Emperor's interest. Inspired, he replied with a letter of his own, and the two began a correspondence. The great man would send her letters of love poems and tales from courtly life, while she replied in kind with letters of her own. They found themselves looking forward to the next letter more and more. Though the two had never met, a bond grew between them.

The princess' life with her parents continued for several years, but after a time, Kaguyahime became very depressed. Her parents repeatedly found her crying under the light of the full moon. At first, they hesitated to ask her about her troubles, but her sorrow grew and grew. Finally, her parents were too worried to refrain themselves from asking. With tears in her eyes, she began her tale.

"I am not of this world. I was born on the moon, and for some reason unknown to me I was brought here to be your child. But I am not of this world, and I am not to be your child forever. During the full moon on the fifteenth day of the eighth month, I will return to the moon."

Her parents were unable to speak for some time. Finally, her father recovered his composure. "I remember the day we found you, and I know you came to us under extraordinary circumstances. I know you grew faster than a normal child, and that you are far more beautiful and graceful than any human I have seen. But you want me to believe you are from the moon?"

"Believe what you will," Kaguyahime said, her voice choked with tears. "But when the full moon comes, I will disappear like a wisp of smoke in the wind." She hugged her parents and they cried until the tears would come no longer.

The princess wrote to the Emperor, telling him she would soon disappear from the earth. The Emperor did not reply, but in place of a letter he himself traveled to the bamboo cutter's home. Over a thousand servants, retainers and officials of the court accompanied him in his journey to at last gaze upon the beauty that was Kaguyahime. The entire entourage arrived on the evening of the fifteenth day of the eighth month.

The moon rose over the mountains just as the procession arrived. A brilliant purple cloud also rose over the mountains, and on it, those who looked closely could see over a hundred maidens each rivaling Kaguyahime's beauty.

The cloud grew nearer to the bamboo cutter's home. As it approached, all those assembled heard a voice as pure and clear as water say "Kaguyahime. Kaguyahime, it is time. Time to come back. Time to leave your mother and father here."

Kaguyahime had by now overcome her sadness and faced the inevitable with calm resignation. "Such was the promise I made before I came. I can only thank you for your kindness over such a long time."

Her parents cried and held her close to them, reluctant to give her up.

"Do not cry for me," she implored them. "But when you look at the full moon, remember me, and remember I love you." Then, she handed them a thick, brown jar. "In this jar is a potion that will keep those who drink it forever young. The magic inside keeps a person who drinks it from aging and protects them from death. Please give it to the Emperor for me."

Then the princess stepped into a small cloud which had developed unnoticed at her feet. The cloud lifted her up to the larger purple cloud. Silently, but with tears in her eyes, Kaguyahime waved as the cloud floated away and took her back to her own world.

The Emperor received the jar from the bamboo cutter, but rather than selfishly use Kaguyahime's gift, he wanted her to know he would remember her long after she left the earth. As his princess had floated away into the sky, the Emperor ordered his retainers to take the jar to the highest point in all Japan—the top of Mount Fuji. There, he decreed, they should place it and its contents in a great sacrificial fire. It would be burnt as an offering to the memory of Kaguyahime—perhaps she could smell the potion as the flames drifted skyward from the mountain top.

To this day, some older Japanese call the evening of the fifteenth of the month *Takehime*, Bamboo Princess.

Japanese Terms and Expressions

Kitsune Nyōbō

Tatami, straw mats used as flooring in many Japanese homes.

Kobutori Jisan

Kobutori is a compound word. A *kobu* is a large lump, usually found on the face. *Tori* is from the verb *toru*, "to take". *Kobutori* is then "taking away a lump".

Jiisan, old man.

The Man Who Brought the Dead Back to Life

Heibō, the name of the main character. The *hei* of his name is a reading of the character for "ash".

Ri, a measure of distance equal to about 3.9 kiliometers or 1.8 miles.

Kasajizō

Kasa, umbrella

Jizō, a stone image of Buddha, often found along roads and in other out-of-the-way places in Japan.

Oshōgatsu, Japan's New Year's holiday season

Mochi, a dumpling of pounded rice.

Kintarō

-chan, a suffix attatched to names indicating a close relationship. (Kin-*chan* is a shortened form of Kintarō-*chan*.)

Sannen Netarō

Sannen, three years

-san, a polite suffix attached to names. *Netarō-san* is something like "Mr. Netarō". Indicates more distance and respect than *-chan*.

Hanasaka Jiisan

Like *kobutori*, *hanasaka* is a compound word. *Hana* means "flower", and *saka* is from the verb *saku*, "to bloom, to blossom".